The Other Side

Ben,

One breath. One Moment. One Step.
Each will get you to exactly
where you are meant to be.
Just never give up.

Yours truly,

JV Manning

Caffeinated Inspirations Publishing Co.

The Other Side

*Where all the life lessons learned from your past
are put to use for a brighter, happier future.*

J. V. Manning

Caffeinated Inspirations Publishing Co.

CAFFEINATED INSPIRATIONS PUBLISHING CO.

PRINTED AND BOUND IN THE UNITED STATES

COVER DESIGN BY J.V. MANNING © 2014
ALL PHOTOGRAPHS AND QUOTES © J.V. MANNING
ALL RIGHTS RESERVED.
ISBN-13: 978-0615957326 (CAFFEINATED INSPIRATIONS PUBLISHING CO.)
ISBN-10: 0615957323

LIBRARY OF CONGRESS CARD NUMBER – PENDING
THE OTHER SIDE / J.V. MANNING
ISBN 0615957323
1ST EDITION

CORRESPONDENCE CAN BE SENT TO:
J.V. MANNING
CAFFEINATED INSPIRATIONS PUBLISHING CO.
P.O. BOX 602
STANDISH, ME 04084

EMAIL: JV@CAFFEINATEDINSPIRATIONS.COM

© J.V. MANNING
WWW.JVMANNING.COM
www.randomthoughtsandlotsacoffee.com

You will get to the Other Side of things eventually.

It may not happen in a way you ever wanted. It may not happen tomorrow. It may break your heart and your spirit in the process, but you will one day pick up those scattered pieces and build a life that you want. That you deserve and that you control. You may need to make some scary decisions; you may need to go out on your own, take some chances and stand firm for what you want, what you need. But, never doubt that you will get there.

Dedicated To:

Laura

Head up. Shoulders back. This is your time. All yours. Make it epic. Believe in the magic you hold inside and trust in your journey. You got this. I will forever be by your side. Love you to the moon.

INTRODUCTION

Not one single soul in this world makes it through life unscathed.

We all have scars, some you can see, some you can't. We all have stories. Stories of perseverance. Stories of strength. Stories of our weakest moments. Stories of when we felt we would shatter from it all. Each of us have moments in life when the sheer magnitude of what we must face drove us to our knees and left us breathless.

We didn't think we could get through it. We couldn't find our way through the darkness.

Some days, we didn't even know if we wanted to.

We lose our light. We lose our confidence. Our heart and soul feel broken. We lose all hope that we can make it through whatever it is we are facing. We do not believe we will ever feel happy or content again.

We don't trust the world.
We don't trust love.
We don't trust tomorrow.

Most of all, we no longer trust ourselves.

So we dig into our unhappiness, mistrust and brokenness. It becomes a safe haven for us. We are already hurt – so bring it on. Until that moment in time when a shimmer of light seeps through our defenses and we want to be better. We want to allow the light to flood back in to scatter the shadows and we desperately want to grasp ahold of the most elusive emotion of all – hope.

Hope for healing.
Hope for love.
Hope for tomorrow.
Hope that we will be ok.
Hope that we will eventually find our happiness.

Hope that our strength and perseverance will bring us through the darkness to the *Other Side*.

We want to make it. We want to believe. We want to dig deep, square our shoulders and face what needs facing, deal with what needs dealing with, and once and for all walk away from the trauma with healed scars that tell our story.

We came. We conquered. We healed.

We made it to the *Other Side* of life. Where all the life lessons from our past are put to use for a brighter, happier future.

Come with me on a journey through these pages and slowly you will see and believe in the possibility of getting through everything you are facing in life. You can do it. You can face it. You can make peace with it. You can heal from it. Then, when you are ready, you will move on from it. I believe in you.

How could I know? Because we are not that different from one another.

Driven to my knees by the burdens life had heaped upon my shoulders, I never thought I would be out from underneath them. I never believed things would get better. I never trusted in tomorrow. I built impenetrable walls around myself, my heart, my soul and shut out the world. I became like a wraith flittering through my days. Devoid of emotions. Broken. I didn't believe it would ever get better; it had never actually been good to start with. I wasn't sure I would even know happy if it ever happened. What I knew was life was coming at me from all sides and I was exhausted.

I would cringe when someone patted my shoulder and told me everything would be ok or that it would work out. Inside I would scream in frustration. I had demons. I had responsibilities that threatened to crush me. Until the moment I realized I would never break simply because I wouldn't allow it.

So, I dug deep each time life hurled something at me and I handled it. Even at my most exhausted and at my weakest moments - I never gave up! I persevered because somewhere deep inside my soul I knew the

Other Side existed and someday, come hell or high water, I would make it there.

For some, it takes years. For others, not so long. For me, it was decades.

It was a lifetime.

I am not really even certain when it happened exactly. One day I just realized I no longer feared what the dawning of a new day would bring. My self-confidence was no longer shaky. I laughed for the sake of laughing. I giggled for no reason at all. I wanted to grow and reach out to others. I wanted to appreciate all that is wonderful and amazing in life. I found my hope. In the future. In the possibilities. In myself.

None of the bad broke me. What it did was strengthen me, made me a warrior. Now I could lay the fight down for a while and instead focus on the good I could do. I could focus on being happy and healthy and adventurous. I was free.

The light came flooding back in, and one day while driving home from work I had the most startling epiphany of all. It was the realization that life may not be done dealing me nasty blows. Bad happens. It is what it is. But I have faced my darkest days and they did not break me. I know now, going forward, nothing ever will. I have earned this peace. I fought like hell for this. I am proud and I am humble.

Allow my words to be the first beam of light through your defenses. Embrace the possibility of reaching your *Other Side* as you walk along with me.

I wish I could hold the hand of everyone working through something, facing something or recovering from something and walk along beside them. But as I have learned, it is often a journey you must do alone. However, trust that you will always find guides to help you when you are ready.

Thank you for allowing me to be one of those guides.

UNRELENTING STORMS

A wild ocean storm was raging. Massive waves violently pummeling the coast as dark volatile clouds rolled in from the east, pregnant with rain. I sat high above, perched on a granite cliff and felt the power of the storm course through my body, torrential rain hiding my tears, and though I was drenched to the bone, I made no move to seek shelter. My heartbeat seemed to match each wave as it crashed against the shore. Dueling storms, outside and within, raged. Tilting my head back, the scream I had been holding in burst out into the wind.

Still the storm raged.
Uncontrollable. Unrelenting. Unapologetic.

Leaning back against the trunk of an ancient pine tree, I could feel the thrashing of the tree's branches reverberate through the bark and into my spine. I closed my eyes and deeply breathed in the briny smell of salt water mixed with the pine needles above my head, creating a powerful scent I found calmed me some, though I could no longer tell the difference between my tears and the rain, nor the wind from my shudders.

After a time, the storm began to subside. The ocean waves slowed their assault on the coast and the storm clouds started to splintered apart, allowing soft rays of sunlight to stream through. Before too long, the only evidence of the storm was the glittering raindrops on the bushes and trees, and the fresh clean scent that always follows the rain. Lifting my face to the sky, I could feel my tears dry, and my shoulders lose some of their tension in the sudden warmth of the sun.

I only wished the storm raging inside my soul would stop just as sudden. However, the conflicting emotions of anger, sadness, loss and confusion still swirl in and around my very being. I stood there on that granite cliff, looking out towards the ocean, and made a silent wish for peace. All I ever wanted was a few stolen moments in time where I felt nothing.

I walked away from the coast that day defeated. I did not believe in happy endings and I sure as hell did not believe things would ever change or that I would make it through all that was so wrong in my life. For better or worse, it was what it was, and I just had to keep dealing with it. I believed whole-heartedly I was not meant to be happy, successful or loved. I chastised myself that day, how could I miss something I had never experienced? This was not a movie and a happy ending was not guaranteed. I knew better. I always knew better. My life was never going to be my own and I just needed to accept that.

This was 20 years ago. I was 16.

I remember this day as if it were yesterday. I remember while driving back to my grandmother's house I contemplated wrapping my truck around a tree. I did not want to live any more. I did not want to face the mountain of problems. I just wanted to be free. Something kept me on the road that day, something I have learned about myself in the ensuing years – I am not a quitter. I am a force and have an innate strength that lives in a remote part of my soul. This part of me would never let me give up. In fact, it made me square my shoulders and yell to the world "Bring it on." I only wish the world had not taken me so seriously.

When I arrived at my grandmother's house, she knew something was up, she also knew that I needed coffee and someone to listen to me. I talked to her and told her everything that was tearing my soul apart, some she knew and some she did not. After I had expunged all of the raging emotions out onto her kitchen table and looked to her for some flash of insight, she told me that everything would work out in time. That things would get better. I just had to be patient. It was the only time I had ever thought her a liar, for I did not believe a word of it. There were no "better days" ahead. There were no rainbows and butterflies and this was not a *Lifetime* movie. This was reality and by now, I had a good handle on what was going to happen. It was going to get worse. It was never going to end and I had to just accept that. I had to give up any dreams I had been foolish to have and simply accept my life as it was.

Now, I look back on my life so far and a sigh escapes my lips. Twenty years have passed since that day. Twenty very, very long years. However, as I sit here today, my grandmother's words ring in my head and I know now what she said was true. Everything does work out in time. In my case, a whole lot of time. My whole life up until the past three years had been one long rolling storm. Filled with strife, loss, anger, devastation, and too many life lessons to count. There had been many times I thought I would break and shatter into a million pieces, but I never did. There were many times when life knocked me down so hard - I thought I would never get back up. Stretches of time when breathing was about all I could accomplish.

It all came to a head a few years ago. The storm that had raged inside of me for as long as I could remember - finally cleared. Life took another completely unexpected turn and all of a sudden, I was through the darkness and into the light I had only dreamed about.

Those first few months, when everything made the sudden shift into new, virgin territory, I was terrified. I could not bring myself to trust in the happy moments, the peaceful stretches and the calm. What life had been for as long as I could remember had shattered into a zillion pieces and for the first time ever, it was up to me to take those shattered pieces of what was and use them to build what will be. It was thrilling. It was exciting, terrifying and so amazing. I had something to prove all right, not to anyone else for a change, but to myself. I could shine now. Nothing was going to hold me back.

I had made it to *the Other Side*. Where all the life lessons I had learned throughout my past could be put to use creating a brighter, healthier and happier future.

My journey, just as yours, has brought us to this very moment in time. We have made it this far and while we most definitely do not want to go back, we can take what we learned into our future. Our future is brighter, happier and more promising than we ever dreamed possible.

I do not know about you, but I never believed *the Other Side* existed. I never believed it was possible.

The Other Side is where your soul takes you after making it through something horrific, devastating, and life changing. It is when the storm clouds part and all of a sudden, life is not something that must be *"gotten through"* and *"survived,"* but something to be cherished and experienced. A time in your life to make good memories, to experience happiness, and contentment. *The Other Side* is where you take all the lessons you have learned from the trials you have faced and put them to use. You stop making the same mistakes over and over again; you begin to trust yourself and your judgment. You allow love to enter into your heart without fear, and you let the most elusive emotion of all back into your life – **hope**.

Take a journey through these pages and let your soul breathe in the possibilities. Change your perspective and change your life. I know what it feels like to be lonely, when it feels like there is not a soul in the world who understands what you are facing and accomplishing every single day. Walk with me and read the words of my soul as it reaches out to you and brings some light into your world. Because no matter how dark it is, the light will always find a way in. Maybe not today. Maybe not tomorrow or the day after. However, eventually, everything is going to be okay. Just never-never-never, give up. Find hope in these pages. Find a crack in your darkness to let the light of my words shine through.

You will get to the Other Side of things eventually. It may not happen in a way you ever wanted. It may not happen tomorrow. It may break your heart and your spirit in the process, but you will one day pick up those scattered pieces and build a life that you want. That you deserve and that you control. You may need to make some scary decisions; you may need to go out on your own, take some chances and stand firm for what you want, what you need.

Never doubt you will get there.

CHILDHOOD REVISITED

Imagine living with the wisdom we have acquired throughout the years coupled with the wide-eyed wonder of the child we once were before life made us jaded.

After my mom died, I discovered two boxes filled with loose photos. Photos that, at one time, had been proudly arranged in albums in chronological order, displaying our lives from birth until she stopped taking pictures of us, which was around my early teen-age years. My mother suffered from Bipolar Disorder. Unfortunately, she never fought the illness and it controlled her. During one of her bad cycles, she had dismantled all of the albums, pulling the photos out and tossing them into a trash can. Hundreds of photos piled up in the can, our lives, our stories and our memories, cast out. Thankfully, when the destruction was complete, my grandmother rescued all of them. Filling these two boxes with the detritus of our lives and hiding them in the basement with all the other mementos that had been discarded during mom's downward spirals.

These boxes have been sitting in my closet since I found them, hidden for the past two years, as I didn't have the mental strength to look at them. Until recently, when for some reason I still do not understand, I brought them out to the light and opened them.

Reaching in, eyes closed, I pulled out the first one my fingers touched upon. Taking a deep breath, I opened my eyes to see what memory I had pulled from the past. The picture had faded over the years, yellowing slightly on the edges, and feeling dry with age in my hand. I sat back in my chair and became lost in this photo of a little girl for what seemed an eternity.

She sits perched on a coffee table, wearing a blue frilly dress and white tights, a pair of soft brown Mary Janes on her little feet, a plastic barrette in her hair and the most innocent big blue eyes. With her hands clasped loosely in her lap, little legs dangling not quite reaching the floor, she looked like a happy child, albeit a bit mischievous, who was quick to giggle and even quicker to make you giggle. I imagine her not sitting still for this photo for very long and loud sighs of exasperation from the one trying to capture the shot.

I stare at this little girl with the big blue eyes and I want to hug her close. I want to whisper in her ear that the road ahead is going to be rocky as hell, but she will make it through. I want to tell her to never lose her giggle and to hold on to the tendrils of her innocence, as life will shred and tatter it. I want to protect and shelter her.

Then I realized - I already had. For the little one in the photo was me.

I don't remember being a child. I don't remember a time when my only cares were chasing butterflies and scattering dandelion seeds on the wind. I don't remember a time when I wasn't facing something, taking care of or protecting someone else, mainly my mom, or keeping things together and shouldering the blame for things I didn't even understand.

I don't remember when I had to put down the crayons and pick up the burdens of life, it seems like they have always just been there. I stare at this picture of a little girl with the big blue eyes and I know her, I just can't connect with her. She is inside of me somewhere, just waiting for her time, but I never bought into the whole release-your-inner-child mumbo jumbo. Well, never before, but now? Now I want to make her proud. Now I want to run through fields and scatter the damned dandelion seeds and chase butterflies.

Okay, maybe not run through fields, but find my giggle - yeah, that would be cool. Rediscover my innocence? I don't even know where to start with that. But what I can do, will do, is live the life I was denied back then - today. I will live the life that little girl worked so hard to give me. She never quit. She never gave up on me. She fought and survived and now, she wants out. That little girl with the big blue eyes, had fire in her soul and so much heart. The world needs her. I need her. That little girl wants to be free.

I find I want to free her. I want to honor everything single thing she accomplished. I want to make her proud. I want to show her everything she faced, conquered, and dealt with was not for nothing. I sure as hell don't want a second childhood, one was enough but what I want - what I will have - is the unfettered joy at simply being alive in this world. What I will do is cast aside the jaded, untrusting, battle scarred woman I was, and become the woman that little girl intended to be before life got in the way.

Imagine living with the wisdom we have acquired throughout the years coupled with the wide eyed wonder of the child we once were before life made us jaded. Seeing each moment, each experience, from this moment forward, as it is and not shadowed by our negative experiences. Imagine waking up every morning and seeing the fresh new day as an adventure and not a chore. Imagine a life where even the simple act of eating a piece of candy, brought forth simple joy. When walking out the door and heading out about your day, we smiled at the sunshine and waved at strangers passing by. Giggling for no apparent reason other than we felt it bubble up and had to let it out.

Imagine taking in the world with fresh new eyes and not the jaded or cynical always-looking-for-problems ones we have now. Imagine taking each moment as it comes and actually living it. We were all kids once. We were all born free and unburdened. Then life interrupted and we lost that spark. The cool thing, now that we are older and wiser, we can rekindle it. We can flame it til it roars! We can take adventures, we can color outside of the lines and we can allow fun to make an appearance in our life. We can honor all those little ones did to get us to this moment - by living out loud. By finding our giggle and losing some of our seriousness.

Ursula K. Le Guin once said; *"Creative adults are children who survived."* This resonated so deeply with me. We see more and understand more because of things we went through. We learned to think outside the box. We are who we are today because of the childhoods we had. We survived. We made it. We learned the lessons; we made our way through and now, well now is when we make up for lost time.

Now is the time we let those kids we were, who got us to this moment, out to play.

LIVE & LEARN

Perfection is a myth.
The only perfect thing about us is our perfect ability to make mistakes.

The other day I was in my kitchen just finishing up lunch. As I got up from the table to take care of the lunch debris, my mind was mulling some things over and I put the milk in the microwave and my leftovers in the cabinet. I would like to say that I noticed my mistake right off. But I can't. Truth be told it wasn't until a few hours later when I went to reheat a cup of coffee that I found the milk. I can't blame a senior moment- I'm not even 40 yet. I can't blame it on anything really, so instead I laughed. A real deep belly laugh and continued on with my day. Wasn't the first time, and sure as hell won't be the last, that I do something so incredibly stupid. Like for instance making a pot of coffee and forgetting to put the pot underneath so that the coffee goes EVERYWHERE. Or forgetting there is a door to my office when I get up to make my way to the copier and walking into it. The door has only been there forever. Or maybe the time when I forgot to put the cover on my travel mug and poured hot coffee all over the front of myself.

Apparently, I am human. Therefore, I make mistakes.

Usually when I have one of my "*Jenn Moments,*" as my husband calls them, it is witnessed by a bunch of people who all ending up laughing- at me. I could berate myself for my missteps; call myself names and beat myself up for being dumb. I could. But I don't. Instead I laugh at myself and shake my head. Swear that I will stop daydreaming and focus more on the mundane tasks I have before me. But I don't.

We are human. Being human means we make mistakes. We trip over imaginary cracks in a parking lot and fall flat on our face. We miss our mouth when eating and get stains on our shirts. Sometimes we forget things. Sometimes we burn dinner. Sometimes we make "grammer erros" and typos when writing or mix word order up because we are thinking faster than we can type. We sometimes say things out loud that we only meant to keep as thoughts and sometimes we put the milk in the microwave instead of in the refrigerator where it belongs.

Sometimes we make mistakes.

Big ones. Little ones. Funny ones. "Oh! No!" ones. Mistakes come in all shapes and sizes. There are relationship mistakes. There are morning after mistakes. There are having too-many-margarita mistakes. The I-should-have-tried-harder-mistakes. There are the blowing your budget mistakes and the fighting with your friend mistakes. The not admitting when you are wrong mistakes. I could go on- but I think you probably get it.

Perfection is a myth. The only perfect thing about us is our perfect ability to make mistakes. We make mistakes that hurt. Sometimes the mistakes we make have some serious repercussions. We make big mistakes that cost us emotionally, mentally, and financially. We regret them. We go over and over what we should have done differently, said differently, and how we could have reacted differently. We second guess everything that led up to the mistake and allow the coulda-shoulda-woulda to take over. We berate ourselves for our mistake. Vow to make it right or vow to never do it again. It eats away at us and causes fear. Sometimes we let that fear take over our minds and control our actions. We allow the fear to stop us from trying again because we are convinced we will make another mistake. We fear saying sorry. We fear owning up to our mistake. Often choosing to walk away from the fallout of what we have done because it is easier then admitting our error. We blame others. We find excuses and in turn; fail to see what it taught us. We fail to see beyond the mistake to how it can make us a better person

Failing to own the mistakes we make is in itself a mistake.

Once I walked out of my house and pulled the door closed behind me. It was locked. No one was home and there I stood on my deck, no shoes on, looking into my home knowing that unless I shattered the window, I wasn't getting back in. I was furious. Furious at the door, the lock and the unfairness of it. I had things to do and places to go. It wasn't part of the day I had planned. I was angry at everything- but myself. I wanted back inside to something that my mistake had locked me out of. I did not have a secret key or magical power to make the situation go away. I wasn't going to break in. I had to suck it up and walk a mile in my socks to where there was a spare key.

I made the mistake. I had no one to be mad at but myself. But instead of standing there wailing at the injustice of it all. I pulled myself up and did what I had to do to make it right. It was painful- walking a long stretch of road with no shoes on. It was humiliating to have to ask for the spare key because of what I had done. But in doing so I was let back in.

Same thing goes with mistakes in life. We have to own them. Stop making excuses and do what we have to do to make it right. We have to laugh at ourselves. We have to stop being so quick to point out the mistakes that others make and focus only on the ones we make. No one in the life is perfect. No one will ever be perfect. So why do you berate and hate on yourself so much when you make a mistake? Making mistakes means that you are living your life. Your life that is not defined by your mistakes. Your life is defined by how you handle your mistakes. Sometimes the mistakes that we make are disguised opportunities. Opportunities to find ways that work, ways to become better or stronger and opportunities to get it right.

Those who can laugh at themselves will never cease to be amused. Those that can own their mistakes and become better for them- will never cease to be respected. Stop beating yourself up when you make a mistake. Learn from it and let it go. Carry the lessons your mistakes have taught you but leave the mistake itself behind.

Live and learn – then let it go.

REALITY CHECK

I have forgiven. I have moved on and moved past so many things. I am proud of how much light I have in my life and how much happier I have become. But I will never be a turn the other cheek kind of woman.

Some of my most philosophical conversations have happened driving down the road. Either running errands, heading to some random destination or just out for a drive. If I am lucky, there is someone else in the truck with me and I am not just talking to myself. Though to be honest, that happens too. I don't know if it is the open road in front of us, the sense of freedom being in a vehicle can give you or the fact that for at least the time you are travelling - you are kinda trapped.

My husband and I got into a pretty deep conversation the other day while driving down the road concerning a comment one of my followers had made on the Random Thoughts Facebook page. This particular comment had stuck with me all morning long and I had been rolling it around in my mind. The comment said - "One of the hardest things in life is learning to love those who have wronged you. To find a place in your heart for them." The comment went on a bit but it was these lines that had me thinking and questioning some truths I hold pretty close. If someone hurts me, wrongs me or someone I love - why in the hell would I want space for them in my heart? Why should I have to learn to love them? I know the whole turn-the- other-cheek-thing but honestly have never bought into it.

So driving down the road I asked my husband a simple (or so I thought) question; "Is there anyone in your world who you hate? Really hate. Not strongly dislike or could do without ever seeing again. But someone who has wronged you or hurt you so bad you can't help but have hate for them?" I explained the comment and how it had me thinking about the roles various people have taken during the course of my lifetime. There have been many angels at one point or another. But there have been a few villains too.

He thought for a while before answering and as the truck was eating up the miles he finally said; no. There wasn't really anyone he hated - really hated. That there was a handful he strongly disliked. A few he would be okay never seeing again. That for the most part if any of them were to come to him and apologize for whatever they did to hurt him; he would probably just let it go. So I went a bit deeper and asked him if he thought he could find a place in his heart and love for the ones who he "strongly disliked?" He kinda looked at me a bit and said; "As with anything in life there are limits."

At this point he turned the question back on me and asked me why this particular comment had my thoughts turning. To be honest, all morning long I had asked myself the same thing. I think it was because it kick-started a self-inventory of where I was at this point in my life. How much I had come to let go, make peace with and move on from? And how much anger and hurt was I still grasping a hold of?

Did I believe I could come to have love in my heart for those who had wronged me? Did I even want to, need to or have to? Did turning the other cheek make me a better person?

My conclusion - No, I don't and no, it doesn't.

I spent some time lost in my thoughts before answering him. I thought about the concept of hate. Of how too much can consume and eat away at you. I thought about the very few people who topped my list of "strongly dislike" and what brought them there. I found that, like my husband, if any of the few who made my list were to come to me and talk about what had happened I would probably be apt to let it go and just move on from it. All except for one.

It was "the one" who had me thinking.

I do not have room in my life for hate and for the longest time I really only felt pity for "the one." That because of the miserable life they had created for themselves, they felt the need to tarnish the lives and happiness of others. Even after countless lines and boundaries had been crossed; it still took me a long time to get to the point of openly admitting I actually hated "the one." But once that line was crossed I had to be honest with myself. I could find no love, no acceptance for this person. They had caused too much damage, too much destruction and caused too much loss. I am human after all and my hate is a valid emotion. It is also an emotion that can consume you if you let it. I refuse to let it take over my life. Instead I choose to honor it. Because it is an authentic feeling and deserved of attention - just as love is.

Who honors hate?

A person who understands there will be people in our lives who hurt us, bully us and push us beyond limits we didn't even know that we had. But they can only break us if we allow it. If we constantly swallow the anger, the hurt and the negative emotions these people cause and let them build and build; we are giving them too much room in our heads. We will eventually break in a rush of built up anger that will serve no purpose. But if we honor the hate we have. Understand it. Make peace with it and grasp it is a valid emotion; an emotion that we do not need to hide or be ashamed of - we in turn release its power.

See where I am going with this?

Stop and ask yourself the same question I asked my husband. "Is there anyone in your world who you hate? Really hate. Not strongly dislike or could do without ever seeing again. But someone who has wronged you or hurt you so bad you can't help but have hate for them?" Be honest with yourself. If you are like him and have just a list of "strongly dislikes"- then awesome. But if you are like me and you have your "the one," the time to confront it is now.

But confront it within yourself. Identify all that led up to causing you to feel this way. Spend some time examining everything this person has done to you. When you feel that rush of anger; let it come. Then as swiftly as you can - let it go. You are not a bad person, you are not a negative person and you are not wrong. If in your gut you feel this, then for you it is truth. Honor it. But at the same time, see it for what it is. An emotion that eventually you may or may not let go of. But you will not swallow it any more. Because by letting it out into the light you diminish its power. Make peace with it and then move on from it.

I have let go so much in the past few years. I have forgiven. I have moved on and I have moved past so many things. I have made peace with the past. I am proud of how much light I have in my life and how much happier I have become. But I will never be a turn-the-other-cheek kind of woman. I know that. I am okay with that. Simply because I value myself, my limits and my boundaries enough to know. I call it self-respect.

Respect yourself.

DON'T LOOK DOWN

Never be afraid of making mistakes. Never be afraid of finding out the wrong way to do or handle things. It wasn't wrong. It was just one step in finding the perfect balance for you and your life. You make adjustments every time you fall.

The woman walks out from behind a curtain and to the center of the arena floor. She is dressed in a sequined suit that twinkles in the spot light. The crowd claps and cheers as she bows and makes her way to a ladder at the far end of the arena. The bright spotlight from above follows her every move. As she begins to climb a hush descends over the crowd - so deep the silence of the thousands of spectators it seems as if they are all holding their breath. When the woman reaches the platform high above the crowd she pauses and collects herself as she sweeps her eyes across the hushed arena. She can feel their fear, their hope and their expectations. Not only will she walk across the entire arena on a tightrope 35 feet in the air, but she will do so without a safety net. The pressure builds and she knows she must go now.

Tentatively she places her foot on the taut metal wire and she begins her journey...

This was a dream I had the other night. I was the woman who walked out into the spotlight and in front of a crowd of people, each with a different expectation of me as I began to walk across the tightrope. Slowly, placing one foot in front of the other I made my way across. Knowing if I should stumble, second guess myself or bend too far to one side I would fall. And there was nothing below to catch me.

I woke up thinking about the dream. To me it represented life and the tightrope that we all walk every single day of our lives. I think a conversation I had with a good friend of mine over coffee the other day is what prompted my dream. She was talking about how she knew she needed to take that first step into the unknown as she begins a new chapter in her life. How she can feel everyone she knows is watching to see if she falls or succeeds in making her way across. Some of the pressure she is putting on herself but some is from the people in her life. She knows she has to take that step. That for her foreseeable future she must juggle life on her own, her children, her new job and face some life lessons. All without a safety net. She is scared of falling.

We have all walked that tightrope of life - trying to maintain our balance while forces outside of our control push and pull us in different directions. Making us struggle to stay on course and not plummet down. However, it's not always outside forces that threaten to knock us off balance.

Sometimes, we do it to ourselves.

Another friend of mine suffers from depression. Life is a daily walk across the tightrope. Too far to the left and she will fall into the depths of despair, and too far to the right leads to manic over the top behavior. Both eventually result in a sudden crash to earth that can take her months to overcome. She struggles every single day to maintain her balance while living her life. She knows it is only she who can control whether she stays balanced and no one can walk that tightrope for her. With each crash and burn teaching her to see what helps to keep her balance and what helps to push her over.

Life is nothing more than a balancing act. And the lack of a safety net is reality. There will be times when you let yourself get out of balance. Focusing too much on the bad so that you get pulled down. Or loading yourself with so many things to juggle you get weary under the weight of it all and it pulls you over the side. But over time and with experience you can learn ways to balance all that is expected of you. You can find ways to balance your moods, your responsibilities - your life. The key component though being you have to take that first step out. You have to still your fear of falling and you have to just get on it.

Never be afraid of making mistakes. Never be afraid of finding out the wrong way to do or handle things. It wasn't wrong. It was just one step in finding the perfect balance for you and your life. You make adjustments every time you fall. You pay attention to what caused you to become unbalanced and you then take the necessary steps to avoid it in the future.

Going through life trying to maintain perfect balance is exhausting. It is so tempting at times to just not even bother. To wallow in sadness and grief. To not pick yourself up because to do so means you may fall again. It cripples your ability to walk without fear of falling if you never even try. Kind of like when a toddler takes first steps. Stand up. Fall down. Stand up. Take that first step. Fall down. Each time getting the hang of how to do it. Same thing goes for you and me. We have to figure out all the wrong ways before we find the one that works for us. But if we never take that first step out onto the tightrope - we can never learn what helps us with our balance.

Like the women in my dream, I know at times it feels like the spotlight light is on you. That the crowds - your friends and family - seem to stare at you expectantly. You have to tune them out and find your own rhythm. Don't bog yourself down in needless things to juggle. Don't bog yourself down with second guessing yourself. Build your confidence with each step. The tightrope gets easier to navigate if you attack it head on. You will get to the other side. Daily as the case may be.

Be your own safety net. Use your strength and your experience to cushion you when you fall. But use your heart and your mind to get back up again. And your courage to begin anew. Knowing in your heart that all the mistakes have only shown you a better way to do it. A more balanced way.

After all, life often resembles a circus. Don't ya think? Some days I think I am stuck in the freak tent myself.

A LEAP OF FAITH

There is nothing to be gained in hiding behind your fear. There is nothing to be gained but wrapping yourself in guilt and sadness. And everything to be gained in releasing it so you can take that leap of faith and build your wings on the way down. There is no shame in laughter, no shame in wanting to allow the light back in.

A few years back a friend gave me a bookmark. On it was a picture of an angel and the quote from Kobi Yamada: "Sometimes you need to take a leap of faith and build your wings on the way down." This is a quote that has stuck with me all these years. Usually popping into my head when I am in the process of talking myself out of doing or starting something that could potentially change my life.

Why are we more often our own worst enemy instead of our own very best friend?

Fear.

Fear of change, happiness, failure or whatever we can conjure up in our minds, which give us an excuse to put the brakes on life's possibilities. If we never take that step then we will never fall flat on our face. We fear the unknown and therefore block ourselves from learning something new before we even get started. We fear letting go of the past and moving on. So we block ourselves and get creative with excuses to justify it. Trying to convince not only the world but ourselves it is the right decision to not take that leap.

But it is not just changing so many are afraid of or trying new things. People fear life itself. They do not trust in it, in their happiness, their abilities or the future. They fear moving on from the past. They fear moving on from love lost, relationships that have ended, their grief or their memories. Simply because moving on from these things will lead them into the great unknown where they could get hurt again and open themselves up to feeling emotions they long ago sealed off in self-preservation. So they draw protective shields around themselves and plant their feet and shroud their life in sadness, grief, anger and frustrations - because these are the only things they trust and believe in.

You become a prisoner of your circumstance. Denying yourself the freedom of releasing it all and taking a leap of faith so you can move on and be happy. Move on and allow the light back into your life. You say you can't. That it is too soon or that you could never open yourself up to the chance. The chance of losing again or exposing yourself to the possibility of getting hurt. You allow the darkness of your fear to take over while holding the key to the chains that bind you the whole time. You are not helping yourself. You are not protecting yourself. You are only short changing yourself.

There is nothing to be gained in hiding behind your fear. There is nothing to be gained but wrapping yourself in guilt and sadness. And everything to be gained in releasing it so you can take that leap of faith and build your wings on the way down. There is no shame in laughter, no shame in wanting to allow the light back in. There is no shame in standing up to what has hurt you, took away your life and rendered you a shell of who you once were. By saying goodbye to it and making peace once and for all with what has happened to you, you turn the key on the lock to the chains that bind you. You begin releasing your fear and you begin making the turn to the light.

The light of your tomorrow.

It is scary releasing your sadness and shrugging off your fear and moving forward. You believe in your sadness and trust in your fear because it feels right. The worst has happened and by not moving on from it, it can't happen again. You hold tight to your feelings of guilt and scoff that you could ever be happy. You have lost so much. It would be a disservice to the one who died. You cringe at the thought of loving again - once burned twice shy. You trust more in the bad that has happened then you ever could in the future of possibilities.

Seriously. Enough.

Your relationship ended. Probably badly, and you have more "love" wounds than you care to admit. Or you lost someone who you loved so much, whose death has rendered your heart empty. You will never smile or feel whole again, you say to yourself. And you won't if you keep stopping yourself.

Release it. Once and for all.

Allow the light back in to your life. Unlock the chains that bind you and LEAP! Release your fear of the unknown and make room in your heart and your life for happiness. Trust that while bad happens - good does too. Know how I know that? Because when you release the fear - You put good back into to the world by simply being a part of it.

Take that leap of faith and build your wings on the way down. You will fly before you know it.

HITTING CURVE BALLS

There are times in life when you either need to acclimate to changes that are out of your control and roll with it or just give up. I refuse to give up. I may get frustrated, sad or tired - but I will continue on.
Quitting is never an option.

There are times in life when something completely out of your control comes out of the blue and knocks you off your feet. You are faced then with a decision. Do you just sit there shaking your head at the unfairness of it or do you get up and figure out what you need to do?

It is in this moment that your whole life can be defined.

You can acclimate to your new situation. Understanding that changes need to be made - you identify what you need to do in order to make it work. Allowing yourself moments of frustrations, fear and sadness, but not for too long. You need to have these feelings and use them to fuel you on. You will make what adjustments are needed in order to continue on with your life.

Or you can quit. Retreat into the darkness and refuse to change, acclimate or fight to adjust to your new circumstances. You tell yourself you are not strong enough, tough enough or that is just isn't worth it. You allow your life to go on auto-pilot and just float through your days as a fallen leaf floats down a stream.

How you handle the curve balls of life not only defines you, it also defines the quality of your existence. Floating through life never touching shore, never planting your feet and never looking up at the sky shaking your fist and saying "Aww hell no - I won't quit!" is taking the easy way out. Don't get me wrong here; floating can be very healing when you are in the immediate aftermath of a curve ball. Grief, illness, job loss or whatever your curve ball is, deserves real emotion and some time to experience it. You have to experience your curve ball, let the emotions flow and NOT hide them, bottle them up or deny them if you ever plan to get past them to the acclimating stage.

The key here is not the deny your fear or sadness with what has happened, but to let it come, let it happen and then let it flow past you as you get ready to begin life anew. It may not be the life you envisioned, wanted or dreamed of, but it is what it is. And that "is" will only be what you make it.

Believe me when I say - I get it.

I feel like I have hit so many curve balls I should quit my job and go play for the Red Sox. It is the out of the blue; never saw it coming ones that get me. Going along minding your own business and BAM! I have been tempted over the years to just swing and miss and take the out. But then I find some part of me refuses to quit and it gives the rally cry and I dust myself off and get ready to come out swinging.

Like now for instance. A little known fact about me - I have junk legs. Since the time when I was 8 years old my knees started dislocating and every day since I have had some level of pain. I acclimated each time they would get worse and continue on. I knew I would never be able to run or jump like the other kids when I was younger or as I got older be as physically active as I would like. But I have always said - it is what it is. I won't let them stop me. Some days are worse than others and I have learned to ignore the pain and try and not let them dictate my life. It has been a long time since they forced me to stop completely and recalculate - until now. Bouncing back is not as easy as it was when I was younger. Now I have to worry about the possibility of not being able to walk for a period of time. I found myself on a Sunday scared and exhausted and having a hard time wrapping my head around it. Then I remembered what I was made of. So I picked up my bat and prepared myself to knock this curve ball out of the park like all the rest. I will handle whatever life throws at me because I can. Because I refuse to quit or feel sorry for myself. Because like all of you - I have worked too hard to get to this point in my life.

This moment in time may very well change my existence. But I will acclimate. I may get frustrated, sad and tired - but I will continue on. As will you.

Quitting is never an option.

TWO STEPS FORWARD - THREE STEPS BACK

Life is going step-by-step. You don't always have to stride, you may take baby steps when you need to, but you must always keep moving forward. Setbacks in life are nothing more than taking three steps back, refocusing, regrouping and then moving on

After working some serious overtime you finally have enough money saved to pay off some bills and buy yourself a special treat, only to have your car break down on the way home from work and have it cost you all you had saved to get it fixed. Or you are doing so awesome on your diet, getting closer and closer to your goal, only to have such a stressful week, you end up cheating and over-indulging and gain back 10 pounds. Or maybe after months of calm in a rocky marriage, something dumb triggers a heated argument, resulting in angry words and hurt feelings.

Two steps forward - three steps back.

It almost seems destined doesn't it? You work so hard and get so close to attaining a goal and then a setback. You are forced to regroup, rethink and start over again. Sometimes even the most minor setback can feel like a gut punch and you are left wondering if it is even worth picking up and continuing on.

A while back I was in physical therapy following surgery on my knee. For weeks I had been working hard to strengthen my leg, get my range of motion back and to be able to walk without crutches. For a time everything had been progressing nicely. After a month I was almost back to full strength, I was walking stronger and for longer periods. All in all pleased with my progress. I was tired of being laid up and ready to get on with my life. Places to go, people to see, and things to do. I was excited. Until, at the beginning of what should have been my last week of therapy,

I pulled my quad muscle and got knocked back to square one. All of my hard work and progress, gone.

Did I want to scream? Yes. Did I get angry and frustrated? Damn right.

Did I give up and quit? Well, no.

What I did was get mad. Then I moved on to sad and frustrated. I was tired of being in pain, tired of being limited on what I could do and so frustrated that I was so close when suddenly, I had to start again.

But it got me thinking.

Setbacks are a part of life. Nothing in life is guaranteed and sometimes we lose. We can bust our ass, give up so many different things in order to attain a certain goal - only to have something break and end up having to take a few steps back to regroup. It feels like the end of the world. It feels like a slap in the face. It makes us question ourselves and why we are even trying in the first place. For some, this is when they throw up their hands and say, "I Quit!" Some let the sadness and defeat weigh heavy on their shoulders, so heavy they can't move forward. While others decided to take a different route and hope for better results.

The key is to keep moving forward. So what if you had a setback? It is life. It is not that you didn't try hard enough. It is not that you didn't give it your all. It doesn't make you weak or any less worthy of attaining whatever goal you are working towards. It simply means sometimes shit happens. Eloquent I know, but seriously, it does.

If you let setbacks throw you off your course, if you let setbacks crush your soul and spirit, you will never get to where you deserve to be. Look for the lesson if there is one. Learn what you can from it. Maybe see a better way of doing things. Then get back up and get back at it. If a stupid mistake caused the setback, shake it off, learn your lesson and get back out there.

Life is going step-by-step. You don't always have to stride, you may take baby steps when you need to, but you must always keep moving forward. Setbacks in life are nothing more than taking 3 steps back, refocusing, regrouping and then moving on.

For moving on is the only way you will reach you goal. Pick yourself up, dust yourself off and get back on the damn horse. Start over if you have to, but start you must. Eyes forward, shoulders back and get over it any way you can.

You are not a quitter.

ACTIONS SPEAK LOUDER THAN WORDS

People will show you exactly who they are, by their actions. They will also show you exactly what you mean to them the same way. Believe them. This is reality. Your reality will be however you decide to handle it.

I got a phone call from a friend gushing about this new guy. She had met him at the local coffee shop a few weeks ago. Casual conversation over steaming mugs of coffee had sparked mutual interest in each other. Both were single, and while neither was actively looking, both realized they would like to get to know each other more. A chance moment had turned into plans to meet again the following day for another round of java and conversing. She went on about how interesting he was, how his stories had her enthralled, and how dashing he was when he smiled. Dimples and all. Not known to be the gushing type - I was slightly amused at my friend. Telling me how much time they had spent together and how excited she was for me to meet him. I was happy for her.

Until I met him.

While the words that flowed effortlessly from his mouth were golden, his eyes never stopped roving the ladies passing by the front window. Continuously checking his cell phone and texting. Spewing forth words of how awesome and how beautiful my friend was and yet he never actually looked at her when he talked. What I saw and what I heard were two totally different things. He claimed to have found the perfect woman for him and yet never stopping his constant appraisal of any female who wandered into his view. He blatantly would stare at his phone while she was talking and never once seemed to actually look at her or really focus on her though she was right in front of him. He talked a lot about himself and yet was completely dismissive when she would tell a funny story about her day or a story of something she and I had done in the past.

His words most definitely did not measure up to his actions.

When I want to get to know someone or I want to know if someone is being honest with me, I listen to their words sure, but mostly, I watch to see what they do. Do they follow through or are their words empty. Do they claim to be a nice person, yet treat some stranger who can do nothing for them badly? Do they make empty promises over and over again and never follow through. Kind of like being a child and asking your parents to go to the park, a movie or something you so desperately wanted to do, only to be told - maybe. Maybe tomorrow. Maybe next week. But the tomorrows and the next weeks came and went and you never made it to that park or that movie.

Words become meaningless if there is no action behind them. It is like the "Yes, Dears" - from a husband to his wife, only he has no idea what he is agreeing to because he is paying attention to the game. It is the "nice guy" who is demeaning and rude to a waitress at dinner or the boyfriend who claims to trust you, yet grills you every time you come home. Empty words, meaningless.

Hold on tight here, I am going to lay some truth down on you - It's not an easy one either. When someone tells you something over and over again, then never follows through - they are simply placating you. Maybe because they don't want to hurt your feelings, maybe because it is just not important to them - but it is placating. One of my biggest pet peeves honestly. I would much rather someone tell me what they actually think and plan on doing, even if it is not what I was hoping for, than have them tell me what I want to hear and hope I forget about it going forward. I don't know about you, but I never forget. People show you their true intentions by their actions. Simple as that. If your wife says to you that she will cut back on her drinking and never does. Well, she really never planned to; she just wanted you off her back about it. If your husband swears he loves you and only you, then you find out he is cheating. He really doesn't love you, nor does he respect you.

Friends who claim to always be there for you, as you are for them, but never seem to be around when you actually need them - are not good friends. Believe in their actions. We must all take the blinders off eventually and see things for what they are. Then do something about it or not. Seriously, you can accept empty words and promises from someone you care about. Just know there will probably be no follow through and your anger or sadness becomes entirely your fault at that point, because you accepted it.

Actions speak louder than words. For words without action become meaningless. Follow through on promises, do what you say you are going to, be the friend you claim to be. Live with integrity and expect it from those you surround yourself with. Trust your judgment, if you feel like the words being spoken will never be followed through on, you are probably right. If the nice guy you met at the coffee shop has a swivel head watching the ladies or if he doesn't call when he says he will - he probably is just not that into you. If your wife doesn't stop drinking to excess and refuses to get help - there is nothing you can do. You cannot help someone who will not help themselves. If you have a child who tells you that she never has homework - and yet is failing half her classes, maybe you should call the school.

People will show you exactly who they are, by their actions. They will also show you exactly what you mean to them the same way. Believe them. This is reality. Your reality will be however you decide to handle it. If you keep getting angry and hurt, but continue to let it go, well then what do your actions say to them?

Will your words be reflected in your actions?

JUST DO IT

There will be times in our lives when we must do something that may hurt emotionally or physically. Moments we will face that will leave scars on our skin or our soul. To me, scars are a sign that though once wounded - you have healed.

I stood there staring at the wall that was about 30 feet in front of me. A big window sits in the center of it offering a view of the woods. I can see the sunlight shining through the budding trees and I want to be in front of that window. I want to feel the warmth of the sunshine on my face and to look out at the trees. But to do this, I must first walk to the wall. I glance down at my feet and will them to move. They stubbornly remain firmly planted on the floor and I feel like a toddler learning to walk, afraid to take the first step because I am sure I will fall down. For a few moments I let my fear paralyze me. My physical therapist stands next to me giving me time and is ready to steady me should I stumble. I have to trust her; which for me is easier said than done. I know I need to take the first step then the next and onward until I reach my goal. My crutches lean against the chair out of reach. I must do this without them. I must find the strength both, physically and mentally, to take these first steps.

So many times in our lives we stand at a precipice to some decision we need to make, something we need to let go of or some life lesson we must weave into the fabric of our lives before we can continue on. Sometimes it causes us to lose our footing and stumble. Sometimes it can paralyze us to the point that we second guess ourselves and in turn let fear plant our feet when we should be moving forward. We may be willing our feet to move but at the same time saying to ourselves "Oh hell no." So we stand there - stuck. Indecision pulled around our shoulders like a cloak we talk ourselves out of what we need to do because we are scared or certain we are doomed to fail or fall down. We over think everything instead of just doing.

We make excuses. We convince ourselves that our indecision is not fear. We doubt our strength and our abilities. We doubt ourselves. We cling to things we need to let go of. We talk ourselves out of decisions that need to be made. We second guess ourselves to the point that we end up going around in circles or worse retreating backwards. We look our goals and our dreams in the face, and convince ourselves we are not strong enough or smart enough or deserving enough to attain them.

We become our own worst enemy.

We know we may need help to get to where we need to be. There are times when our stubbornness and refusal to ask for this help hurts more than our pride. It can hurt our minds and our bodies. To ask for help means we see ourselves as weak and if you are like me; I would sooner poke myself in the eye than admit I need help. Never showing weakness has served me well throughout my life and I have always handled what life threw at me. Handled it, dealt with it and moved on from it. But as I have gone through a month not being able to walk, not being able to do much of anything because of my injury I found myself faced with a life lesson I never saw coming.

Couple of them actually.

The first one was that in order to make it through this injury - I was going to need help. I was going to have to admit to myself, putting my pride aside; I couldn't do all of this on my own. The second lesson I have learned is that I must trust in the ones who are helping me. And the third lesson I learned was in order for me to walk again, I must inspire, encourage and be my own best friend. I must still my doubts. I must still the fear of falling and pain. I must dig deep and I must force myself forward.

There will be times in our lives when we must do something that may hurt emotionally or physically. Moments we will face that will leave scars on our skin or our soul. To me, scars are a sign that though once wounded - you have healed. It will not happen overnight, but it will happen.

Asking for help or allowing someone to stand next to you should you stumble is not a sign of weakness; it is a sign of true strength. Even the strongest of people have to set their burdens down for a while. Trust in those who step up to carry it for you and remind yourself that you will pick up and carry on again soon. But for now you will trust in the goodness and the strength of another to get you to where you need to be.

Stop giving up. Stop making excuses. Stop babying yourself and convincing yourself that you are not strong enough or smart enough to do what needs doing. Stop talking yourself out of decisions and learn to follow your gut. Learn to inspire yourself. Put the brakes on over thinking everything and learn to simply do. Simply act. Set your sights on where you need to be, on what you need to do, plan out your steps and then - GO. Trust in your initial decisions, don't over think it and when it hurts or the pain becomes almost too unbearable - dig a little deeper. Encourage yourself instead of berating yourself. Challenge yourself instead of always walking the safest and straightest route. Be more of you than you ever thought possible and then go further.

I stood there for a few moments staring at that wall. I stopped myself from thinking of all the reasons why I shouldn't take the first step. It could hurt. I could fall. I may not make it to the wall. But then I realized it would hurt me more to not even try. Sure it would probably hurt and I may be a slow as a turtle - but it would be far more damaging to give up. I owed myself encouragement. I owed myself to suck it up and just do it. I may fall, so what. I will get back up. It may hurt, so what. I will heal eventually. I couldn't force my feet to move - I had to simply allow them the freedom of going forward.

I squared my shoulders, relaxed my mind and went on intuition. Those first few steps without the support of my crutches were terrifying and liberating all at the same time. Sure it hurt, but the relief of finally being on my way to healing overpowered the pain. My confidence grew with each step and I made it to the wall. The sun shining through the window could not have felt any sweeter. As it will be with whatever you are facing - trust in those who want to help you. Inspire yourself to get to where you need to be.

LIES AND THE PEOPLE WHO BELIEVE THEM

The gut-punch life lesson I learned at an early age... people will believe horrible things about you because it makes them feel better. It makes them feel superior. Especially if you are a successful, well rounded person. Stop defending yourself to people who didn't give it a second thought when they judged you.
They don't deserve it.

It was the middle of August and the air was heavy, hot and humid. I remember wanting nothing more than to be sitting on my special rock next to the ocean, drinking iced coffee and feeling the cool ocean breeze. Instead, I was on my hands and knees scrubbing a bathroom floor. Wasn't even my bathroom, it was my mom's. I remember being hot, tired, frustrated and feeling like Cinderella with an evil step-mother.

My mother in the meantime was in the living room on the phone with one of her friends. Sitting near a fan and drinking iced tea, she was lamenting about how awful and useless her daughters were. How they did nothing to help her out, gave her nothing but trouble and was just horrible to her every day. She would pause here and there during the conversation and sniffle at the injustice of it all. I could hear this from my position on the bathroom floor with a cloud of chemical cleaners surrounding my head and sweat pouring down my back. I remember closing my eyes and trying to still the rising sadness in my mind. This wasn't the first time I had heard her go on like this, wouldn't be the last either.

It didn't matter that I paid her mortgage for years, or that I worked 50 - 60 hours a week. It didn't matter that I cleaned her house or sat there and listened to her problems for hours after working a 14-hour day. Never mattered that my sister and I paid her bills, bought groceries and handled her ever-increasing instability, when she talked to her friends, other family members or really anyone who would listen, we were horrible creatures.

Thing is, she was believable. Even to me and I knew better. I learned speaking up and defending myself or calling her out on her lies, never made a difference. I also learned people will believe whatever someone tells them if they want to and nothing you say to counteract it will be believed.

So, I stopped defending myself.

If people wanted to think the worst about me with never having actually talked to me - I let them. I didn't need them nor did I want them in my life. Sure it hurt like hell, it made me question everything I did and how I handled every situation I came across. Maybe I wasn't doing enough, maybe they were right. So I did more. It was when that still it wasn't enough that I finally realized - this is just how life for me was going to be. Some people regardless of how well you think you know them, love them or trust them – will believe everything told to them that makes you out to be a horrible person. Don't ask me why. It just seems to work out this way with certain types of people.

Being lied about is horrible in itself. But I think what is worse is when someone lies about you to someone in your life and this person believes it without ever coming to you. Recently, this subject has come up with a couple of friends of mine. One woman's reputation was attacked by a supposed "friend" for reasons no one can seem to figure out. In a grown up game of telephone - this "friend" had gone to various mutual friends and spread made-up stories. This act in itself was hateful and heartbreaking to my friend. She hadn't done what this woman had claimed, not only was she not the type, but she wasn't even around when she was supposedly doing these things. But there were a few people who believed the stories. They took them at face value and completely allowed it to change their perception of her. She was labeled a troublemaker, a liar and a fraud. She lost friends because of one woman's stories that were nothing but fiction.

To me, this speaks more about her friends who believed it, than to the one who started it. When she and I talked about it - my reaction was, well now you know who your true friends are. Because your friends are the ones who will always believe in you. Or come to you first before just believing a random story, to get your side of things. Not just cut you off, judge you and tell you how awful you are. I told her she didn't need people like that in her life. She is a tremendous woman. Her integrity is solid; she is caring and wonderful person. People who would believe anything less do not deserve a place in her world. She is worth so much more than that.

Another friend had a similar situation when a co-worker was spreading lies about him at work. This co-worker was upset with my friend and decided that he would get him back by telling anyone who would listen, how much of a jerk he was, how he never stood up for his employees and was awful to work for. People believed him. When it got back to my friend, a guy who pours his heart and soul into his work, who treats his workers like family, he was heartbroken. Not so much at what had been said - but more so because of what had been believed. He was devastated to think people who knew him - would ever believe such stories.

The gut-punch life lesson I learned at an early age - people will believe horrible things about you because it makes them feel better. It makes them feel superior. Especially if you are a successful, well rounded person. Stop defending yourself to people who didn't give it a second thought when they judged you. They don't deserve it. And they probably won't believe you anyway. If someone is spreading lies about you, telling stories and starting rumors and some people believe them without first coming to you directly - well you don't need them in your life. It is their loss. For not taking the time to see for themselves. For not taking the time to make their own judgments based on their own perceptions and for being so quick to think the worst of you. Truthfully, they weren't really good friends or family, for that matter, to begin with.

People who love you and who cherish you are ones who believe in you. Who take the good and the bad and love you for both. True friends will defend you, stand up for you and come to you first. The ones who spread lies about you, tell untrue stories and make you out to be something you aren't, for whatever reason, obviously are not your friend. But neither are the ones who believe the stories, rumors and untruths. It will break your heart when these people show their true colors for sure, but remind yourself that you deserve to be surrounded by authentic friends and family. And though it may hurt for a while - you will be better off without them.

Never for a moment doubt yourself because of another's dishonesty. Stop spending time defending yourself to people who were so quick to believe the worst and surround yourself with authentic friends who see and love you for who you are. People who have seen you at your worst and at your best, and love you without fail.

It hurts so much when you hear how certain people feel about you. It hurts when someone has formed an erroneous opinion about your character without ever really getting to know you. The real truth of the matter is - it really isn't about you at all. It is more about them, their view of the world, their own lack of self-esteem, and their inability to form their own judgments.

Some people in this world will just not like you. So what? Spend time and thoughts on the ones who do. For it is those who will walk beside you throughout life. Focus and believe in those who always believe in you. The rest do not deserve your time, thoughts or energy.

They do not deserve **YOU.**

Ups, Downs and All Arounds

I promise you, regardless of how dark everything seems right now, how overwhelming and completely unsolvable your problems and stresses feel - you will eventually get through them. May take days, may take weeks or like me for some of them - years. But you will get there. You will always get there and you will be a better and stronger person for it.

Life is like riding a roller coaster. Blindfolded.

You feel it moving, speeding up and slowing down, you feel it climbing at times - working hard and feel it suddenly plummet as it makes a crest over some huge hill and you are suddenly sailing through the air. You can't see what twists and turns are coming or prepare for the sudden depths that your car plunges, only to even out when you least expect it. The only options you have are to hang on or throw your hands up to the sky and roll with it. You can't fight it. You can't jump off and you can't pause the smooth sections as hard as you may try. You may wish you could stand on the platform for a while, catch your breath and just watch as the empty car travels along without you - but you can't. Life does not come with a pause button.

On the roller coaster we call life; there is only one direction you can go. Forward. There is no chance of reversing; no going back and side to side is never an option. Where you came from doesn't matter nearly as much as where you are going. But, like life, your view of what is in front of you will not become clear until you get there. You can prepare yourself as best you can, as long as you are looking forward. But if you are constantly looking back to where you came from - you just might miss what is in front of you when it comes.

You can never go back. Sometimes I think this is one of the hardest lessons people learn. You can never go back. You cannot undo certain things and while most are tempted to hold on as tightly as possible - once something has ended, you have to move on. Otherwise you are left clinging to memories and to ghosts that are shadows of a part of your life that is over. You have to keep going forward - regardless of how scary the thought of it can be.

Life is fluid.

Someone once said to me during a particularly difficult period in my life *"everything will work out."* I remember looking at them and sighing. A sigh loaded with defeat and sadness. I asked them when. When would everything be okay? When would life magically work out? How in the hell could it possibly ever be anything but a struggle? I was dealing with so many different things at the same time, for so long - I was overwhelmed and exhausted. I look at them and angrily told them not to give me platitudes. I didn't need any flowery phrases or inspirational gobbly gook. What I need was a break.

Now sitting here years later I realized something. Everything does eventually work out. Maybe not in the way you wanted. Maybe not in the way you envisioned it. But it does. As I sit here looking back over a number of moments in my life that at the time I could never see my way through to the other side of, I realize each and every one of them are over. Some I would love to have ended differently and some I wish I could do over completely - but they are over and I am still standing. Weary maybe. Slightly jaded and possibly a little more neurotic then I was - but still standing.

So it is with whatever you are facing in your life right now. I know it feels like your problems and circumstances will never change. That things will never get better or you will never find your happy again. That the "everything will work out" phrase is nothing more than inspirational bullshit and maybe it is. Maybe life doesn't actually ever work out. Maybe it just acclimates and readjusts to our changing circumstances. But I promise you, regardless of how dark everything seems right now, how overwhelming and completely unsolvable your problems and stresses feel - you will eventually get through them. May take days, may take weeks or like me for some of them - years. But you will get there. You will always get there and you will be a better, stronger person for it. You will know, without any shadow of a doubt, you can handle anything and everything life throws at you.

You will see eventually all the crap you have gone through, are going through or will be going through - will try you, it will test you and it will do everything it can to break you. But if you trust that eventually it will work out somehow and you will get to the Other Side, none of it will break you. Like being on a roller coaster - you take what comes your way. Throw your hands up and scream when you need to, or cover your eyes and hold on tight - but keep looking forward, because the next sudden twist could lead you into something amazing that you never thought possible. The next turn could be your turn. Your turn for happy. Your turn for success. Your turn to make everything okay in your world.

As Robert Frost once said,
"In three words I can sum up everything I've learned about life –
It goes on."

As will you.

You are strong enough to see yourself through whatever it is you are facing. You are strong enough to fight to get to where you need to be. You are strong enough to see the *Other Side* of life. Never doubt that for a minute. Trust that eventually everything will work out. Promise.

NEWSFLASH! MEN ARE HUMAN

Men need to realize they are human. Men need to realize it is acceptable to feel sad, overwhelmed and at a loss as to what to do. They need to understand this does not make them weak. It does not make them any less a man. In fact it shows their strength. Because it takes guts to admit when you are not okay. It takes courage to reach out and say, "I need help," and it takes balls to do something about it.

You arrive home from work tired and stressed and wanting nothing more than a warm bath, glass of wine and quiet. Instead you are greeted by a sullen husband, screaming kids and a dog who acts as if he hasn't seen you in months. Your husband calmly listens as you describe your day - in detail. He grunts a few times in response and you suddenly feel like he is upset with you. You asked the question every man dreads and very few actually answer, "what's wrong with you?"

You get the standard answer of "I'm fine" as he walks away. You spend the rest of the evening worrying it over in your mind. The, is-he-angry-doesn't-love-me-anymore-I've-done-something-wrong litany goes in circles in your exhausted head and you get frustrated and sad. The next day you reach out to your best friend and talk to her about it. When you get home the next afternoon you sit him down and demand he tell you what's wrong. He gives you an angry response of nothing, tells you that if you keep asking him "what's wrong" - something will be wrong. The conversation goes downhill from there, and you both retreat. You feel like he is hiding something.

He knows he is hiding something. But, it's not even close to what you are thinking. He is hiding the simple fact that he is sad. That he is overwhelmed with the stress of life and he doesn't know what to do. He loves you with everything he has. He loves his family and would do anything for them. Except for reasons he can't put his finger on - he feels like his is failing. At being a good husband, a good father, a good provider and a good man. He is facing a slew of emotions that to him are unmanly.

They make him feel weak and that in turn makes him angry. Not at you. Not at the kids or the dog. Not really at the guy going the speed limit in front of him. Anger is a manly emotion. It is an accepted emotion for a guy. A man knows tears, sadness and depression are something he can never admit to. Never show. Not to you, not to his friends and most of all, not to himself.

Over the past couple of weeks I have received four messages from four different men, each coming from different parts of the country, different backgrounds and different living situations. Two were married, one was living with his girlfriend and one was single. All of them feeling worthless, lost, depressed, and overwhelmed. None of them knew what to do. They felt like they couldn't talk to their wives, friends or family. They were angry, alone and confused. They felt isolated because men are supposed to be strong, confident and good providers. Each admitted their anger was out of control and one had been contemplating suicide. In communicating with these guys I realized something. How much pressure men are under. From society, from other men, but mostly, from themselves.

We all know the stereotypes. Women are talkers, women are emotional beings and it is perfectly acceptable to cry whenever we need to. Society expects it, is okay with it and finds nothing wrong when a woman shows her feelings. On the other hand, men are not talkers. Men are doers, they are stoic creatures and they are strong. They are the protectors, the providers and are for the most part, emotionless. They can be happy, for that is accepted. They can show anger and dominance, for that is accepted too. Men are programmed from childhood - be tough, don't cry, never show weakness and appearance is everything. If they fail at any of this - then they are weak.

So they bottle up their emotions. Push them down to the dark recesses of their soul and ignore them. But, over time these emotions build up. Stress triggers health issues, they pull away from loved ones, they work insane hours, and accuse their wives/girlfriends of not loving them anymore. Instead of talking about what they are feeling, they project their emotions onto to those closest to them. The kids get the anger; the wife gets shut out and yelled at. They feel like everyone around them sees exactly what they are hiding and thinks less of them.

They feel isolated and simply not good enough.

In the U.S. men are four times more likely than women to contemplate suicide. Many men get so overwhelmed with social problems - being out of work, not making enough money, feeling like they are not a good provider, that it builds up and up and they really have no outlet for what they are feeling. Everyone knows life can be stressful, overwhelming and completely unfathomable at times. But this is especially true if one does not have a way to get it out of themselves. To talk about it, identify what exactly they are feeling and own their emotions.

Men need to realize they are human. Men need to realize it is acceptable to feel sad, overwhelmed and at a loss as to what to do. They need to understand this does not make them weak. It does not make them any less a man. In fact it shows their strength. Because it takes guts to admit when you are not okay. It takes courage to reach out and say, "I need help," and it takes balls to do something about it.

Men also need to realize they are not alone in this. That at some point in every man's life feelings of inadequacy and weakness have arisen. At some point every other man on this planet has been where they are now and there are so many there right now.

They need to realize the only way they will become a failure, to their families, to their children and most importantly to themselves - is if they continue to do nothing.

Secret's out; men have emotions. We must support them and listen to them, just as we want them to listen to us. We must not belittle their emotions and try to understand them. This honestly, is more often than not harder than understanding women's emotions.

Men... Own your life. You will be better and stronger for it. Promise.
But do something. Never give up.

THERE'S NO EXPIRATION DATE ON DREAMS

Never let anyone steal your dreams. Never let anyone tell you that you are not good enough. That you are too old, too dumb and too busy. Most important of all - stop telling yourself that. Own them. Stop over-thinking and finding all the reasons why you can't and start finding reasons why you can.

For a moment, I want you to close your eyes. I want you to silence the world around you and take three deep cleansing breaths. I want you to forget for just a moment everything you have waiting. The chores, the life demands, obligations and minutia of your life. I want you to take a trip back to the place in time when you first discovered your dream. The moment something triggered such a response in your soul that you knew, without a shadow of a doubt, this was what you wanted for your life. A time when you discovered something that intrigue you, fired you up and had you dreaming of the possibilities. Was it the first time in a kitchen when you created something from scratch and knew right then and there you wanted your own restaurant? Was it the moment you taught a lesson to a child and knew teaching was your calling? Was it back when you were a child and the call you felt to be surrounded by animals, knowing you were meant to heal, and take care of them? Or in the way you always knew just what to do when a friend skinned their knee and you rushed to care for them?

Close your eyes and remember.
Remember for a moment your dream.

Now, hold that in your mind. Notice what you are feeling. Pride because you are living it? Sadness because you lost it somewhere along the way? Nostalgia of a time forgotten? Anger because circumstances and life just never went your way? Or maybe remembering made you laugh. I mean who hasn't dreamed of flying into space or joining the circus at some point?

But maybe, just maybe, you are feeling motivated. Motivated to pick up your dream, dust it off and give it a go.

Ever since I was a little girl I dreamed of being a writer. I would write short stories, poems, articles and notes, every chance I got. I believed in my dream. I felt it in my very soul that writing was exactly what I was supposed to be doing. I didn't understand the importance of my dream. I didn't understand what it meant for me. I didn't understand that life and people would try to smash my dream, would belittle it and would ignore it. When I was young I believed in my dream and I believed in myself. It just seemed natural.

But as the years flew by and I grew up - both life and reality took its toll. I started to believe in the nay-sayers. I started to question my abilities. Life took over and I found myself further and further away from my dreams. I became a caregiver in my family, the peace keeper and found year by year that creative spark that had flowed so naturally, diminished. Reality had put a damper on it. Reality at times had completely blown it out and I was left playing the hand I had been dealt. I thought at the time I had no choice. No say in the matter. I had life to deal with. My dreams would have to wait.

Thing is sometimes dreams do have to wait. Sometimes we have to walk our paths and do what we must. Sometimes we have to place our dreams on a shelf and raise our children, work, care for aging parents and make our way in life. But, we must never let their flame go out. We must visit them every chance we can and remember. And one day, we must make the decision to own them. To bring them down and dust them off and make them happen. Or at least try.

Maybe they have evolved since the time when we first had them. Maybe they have grown and matured right alongside us, only we never knew. Maybe just maybe, with a little soul searching and tweaking we can make them into reality. But first we must get back in touch with them. We must remember our dreams. We must allow ourselves the freedom to dream them, to feel them and to imagine the possibilities. We must silence the fear. We must silence the nay-sayers and stop finding all the reasons why they couldn't possible come true. You are not too old. You are not unworthy. So what if your life is a mess? So what you are scared?

You are never too old. You are never unworthy. Life is always messy, and being scared is natural. Use your fear to motivate you. Put yourself out there in a way you never imagined possible and go for it. Release your dreams. Release the feeling of regret and focus instead on the feeling of what if?

Back in 2011, I was just shy of 33 years old. I was beaten down, exhausted and just floating through the days. Life had been hellish, draining, and all I wanted to do was hide. I needed to get all the negative out of myself. I sat at my kitchen table one day, drinking coffee and utterly lost. So much bad had happened. I was realizing how much of my life had been spent living for another. How much of my life had been about everyone but me. I was at a crossroads and had no idea which way to turn. My dreams all but forgotten. I reached for a pen without even thinking and started writing. Words flowed from my pen as if it was possessed and I began to remember. I didn't stop to analyze, I didn't over-think it and I simply let it flow

That day, I built a website and added a blog, which in turn inspired a Facebook page. I wrote from a place inside of myself that I had all but forgotten existed. It was like running into an old friend who you haven't seen in a long time. Only this time I was running into myself. I wrote and published pieces with no end game in sight. I had absolutely no idea what would come of it. But the need to create again, the need to have words flowing was so strong; I knew I could not deny it.

The nay-sayers came in full force. Trying to tell me what I could and could not write about. Trying to stop my dreams from going forward. For the first time in my life I fought back and said no. Not this time. This time I fight for my dreams. This time I will see where it goes and I will not let anything or anyone - stop me.

In 2013, I published my first book. Never in my life have I felt so validated. Never before had I felt the pride holding that book in my hands brought. I had forgotten what hope felt like and holding that book, my book, reminded me.

Never let anyone steal your dreams. Never let anyone tell you that you are not good enough. That you are too old, too dumb and too busy. Most important of all - stop telling yourself that. Own them. Stop over-thinking and finding all the reasons why you can't and start finding reasons why you can. Your dreams are not silly. Your dreams are not unattainable. Your dreams may have been forgotten but you can remember them. You can reignite them.

Your dreams are waiting. Go after them.

IT IS WHAT IT IS

Though you had no control over what happened and though it is not your fault and you never asked for it to occur - it is your responsibility to put the pieces back together and make yourself whole once more.

A few weeks ago I was asked to be on a radio show for a local station here in Maine, to talk about my work, my new book, life and whatever randomness we came up with. I was honored and agreed to do the show. The hostess asked poignant questions about my writing, my thoughts and of course about my love of coffee.

At one point we were talking about the things I write. About how I take what I have gone through in life and use my experiences to fuel my words. When she asked about my feelings on all I had gone through and all I had to face during the course of my life so far, my response to her was simple - it is what it is.

It is what it is.

I have taken responsibility for my life, my actions and my reactions. I have taken responsibility for the past, the present, and the future. Sounds so simple but yet when you stop and look around you, taking responsibility for anything is a foreign concept for most. No one wants to own their mistakes. No one wants to admit when they are wrong and no one wants to step up and say, "Hey yeah that was me and I will take care of it."

Not in politics, not at work and most importantly, not in our own lives.

It is within our own lives that taking personal responsibility is so important. Yet, it is one of the last things a lot of us ever do. Whether it is dealing with your past, facing addictions, leaving a loveless marriage, facing circumstances that were out of your control, or where a bad decision or a slew of bad decisions that landed you in a place you never saw coming. Never once imagining your life could end up where it has -

and instead of examining all it took to get you there, you blame everyone else, throw your hands up and say, "Not my fault."

If it has to do with your life, regardless if it was outside forces initially that got you where you are today, it is totally on you for not doing something about it now. It is your fault if you spend more time placing blame and lamenting on all that is wrong, with little to no time doing something to correct it. It is your fault if you do not take the necessary steps needed to actively heal your mind or body; to not seek help or to allow yourself to simply wallow in the unfairness of it all. Sometimes life is unfair. Sometimes something will happen and knock you to your knees. Of course you could stay down there – but do you really want to?

It is what it is.

There are so many things that happen in life we simply just cannot control. Growing up for me was a series of events that I had zero to do with. But yet it affected every facet of my life whether I wanted it to or not. I could come up with a very solid litany of reasons why I couldn't possibly be happy, couldn't possibly go on, couldn't possibly be a well-adjusted adult, and most of them would be valid reasons. But I won't. It is what it is and there is not a damn thing I can do to go back and change any of it - but I can take responsibility for my now, I can say, "Yes a lot of bad happened. Yes it helped make me who I am today. Yes it hurt and sometimes the ghosts of those memories haunt me, but I will not let them control my emotions, my life or my future."

While I may not be able to take responsibility for what transpired, I damn well can take responsibility for the effects it has on my life today. Do I want to be a shrunken shell of a human? Do I want to be afraid of taking chances? Do I want to be sad and miserable and hate the world?

Ummm, no. Make that a **Hell No!**

I want to own my life. This means taking responsibility for it.... All of it.

Don't get me wrong here; I have made my fair share of mistakes. Typically my mistakes are pretty colossal - epic is a good word and I would like more than anything to blame them on someone else. Like when I was 16 and started smoking - after years of watching every family member I had light up, it seemed like the thing to do. It wasn't. I knew all the warnings, knew all the health risks and with no one forcing that Marlboro into my mouth I still decided lighting up was a good idea. Do I blame the smokers in my family? Nope. Because I made that choice. Have I quit yet? Nope. Whose fault is that? Mine again. Every time I fail at quitting - initially finding any excuse that seems plausible at the time (it isn't) it is my fault for giving up. Not the stress, not someone firing me up and making me angry or whatever - it was that I simply gave in and smoked another one.

Death. Divorce. Job loss. Abuse. All are tragic events that can happen, sometimes without warning. All elicit some serious emotional and physical trauma in life. Losing a loved one can be like losing a part of your soul, the breaking up of a family can be devastating, losing your financial means is scary and recovering from any type of abuse can be earth shattering. You had no control over what happened, and it is most definitely not your fault - it is what it is. It happened. It was one of the bleakest and darkest moments of your life. And though you had no control over what happened and though it is not your fault and you never asked for it to occur - it is your responsibility to put the pieces back together and make yourself whole once more.

Is it fair? No. Is it necessary? Yes.

It can also be extremely empowering when you suddenly realize that you do have control, especially after feeling like you have lost all of it. Because, you do have control. You have control to pull yourself up. To face what has happened and to make peace with yourself. Sure, you may stumble and fall a few times, but don't look around for excuses. Instead pick yourself up and vow to begin anew. As many times as it takes until you get to where you want to be.

So what if you make a mistake? You are human. So what if you don't get it right the first time? You are healing. So what if you are alone and scared?

You will begin to discover that you are your own best motivator when the end result is a happy and content life. You owe it to yourself to take full responsibility in getting there. No one else has that power, except for you. Harness it and do what needs doing. Stop finding excuses for all the reasons why you can't and start finding all the reasons you can. Embrace your responsibility to yourself. Own your life and all of your experiences. Dig deep; face your fears and your sadness.

If you do all of this. If you take personal responsibility for your life, I promise you, one day your answer to a question about all you have faced in your life will be —

"It is what it is - and it did not break me."

FEELING SNARKY

If you are like me you have had many moments where if you had bitten your tongue any harder to keep the words from falling out of your mouth, you would have bitten it clean off.

Snarky. The Urban Dictionary defines snarky as meaning short tempered or irritable and I find this definition apt for my mood the past couple of weeks. I do not like to write when I feel snarky, as I have a tendency to rant and no one needs to read that. But then I got to thinking, how many times in your life have you felt snarky and for good reasons, only to keep your mouth shut about it so as not to ruffle any feathers? Probably a lot. Probably too much. If you are like me you have had many moments where if you had bitten your tongue any harder to keep the words from falling out of your mouth, you would have bitten it clean off.

I am not by nature an irritable, short-tempered person. But, I find there are certain types of people, certain situations and certain things in life that bring the snark out of me whether I want it to come or not. Things that never fail to bring out the snark - people who cannot grasp the concept of responsibility and people who blame everyone else for their misfortunes. I also find I have no patience for power trips and people who feel that putting others down, making up stories about or disrespecting others, somehow makes them more important than anyone else. I also tend to get irritable when life has me running in a thousand directions and I can't squeeze in time to write, more so when it is because others are not doing things they are supposed to and in turn forcing me to handle things that I shouldn't have to.

But that's life, right?

Sadly, yes at times it is. Doesn't mean I have to like it. Doesn't mean I have to keep quiet about it either. Each and every one of us gets snarky and each one of us knows our triggers too. The question is how to handle them.

One of my biggest triggers is when someone will not take responsibility for their own life. The person who spends more time complaining about things, circumstances, their health, finances or whatever, and no time actually doing something about it. The person who blames everything and everyone else for all that is wrong with their life and never stops to think, "Hey maybe if I changed this, worked more, or fixed myself, my life would get better." What I have learned is no matter how hard you try, how much you do or support you offer, you cannot help someone who refuses to help themselves. Also, and this is a big thing, if you keep doing, fixing, taking care of everything - they will never do it on their own. Why would they? So simply put - stop. Just like that. Maybe they step up and handle their own life, maybe they find someone else. The point being it will no longer be you.

Another trigger for me is people who constantly put people down, lie about others and try to discredit people they view as a threat. Call them haters, call them doubters, call them bullies or whatever, the hate they spew speaks volumes - not about you, but about themselves.

I was talking to a girlfriend the other day who is dealing with a situation with a woman who is constantly spreading lies about her. She doesn't even really know this woman but has to deal with the fallout of what she is saying all the time. She was irritated at the fact that nothing seems to stop her from running off at the mouth. Nothing she did, nothing she said was going to stop this woman from trying to discredit her. I just looked at her and said; "Is what she is saying true, no. Are you speaking up for yourself when confronted with her lies, also no. So, what you need to do, is call her out or make sure the people who matter know the truth, and just let it go." She looked at me kinda funny when I said the last part. But here is the thing - You cannot control the actions of anyone else in this world. You can only be responsible for you. Your reactions to this type of behavior will dictate the quality of your life. Make sure those who need to know the truth about you or a certain situation do and then walk away.

People who spread lies and rumors about you - are not your friend. Even if they were at one point, they aren't once they do this. You don't need them and you don't need their crap in your life. It is entirely up to you to walk away. Use your power and deny them the ability to affect you, hurt you or control how you live.

I don't like feeling snarky. This feeling tends to block my writing muse, make me tired, snappy and all around cranky. I really don't like feeling cornered by the actions of others either. I find that when I am being forced to put up or shut up about circumstances that are not at all what I want or need in my life, the snarky tends to ratchet up a few notches. I know I need to work on having more patience with certain types of people and situations. No one and nothing in life is perfect, me included, which means having patience with myself, too. All of which is easier said than done most days.

Often, I have to learn, relearn and re-relearn that while I may not be able to control how certain people act, I can control how I react to them. I also need to learn that if I am constantly running in circles and never seeming to have enough time - it is MY personal responsibility to see that I get the time I need. If that means leaving the dishes in the sink or a messy living room, so be it.

I am also learning - it is entirely okay to put yourself in a time out. To put everything down for however long you need and walk away to get your head straight. If other people don't understand, well then, that is their problem. If you are feeling overwhelmed, over-tired and just damn plain old snarky - put yourself in a time out. Figure out what is causing you to feel this way and then, do something about it. Remember it is you who holds the control over your life, stop giving it away to everyone else.

For the record, I have also found screaming into pillows occasionally helps to relieve some tension, as does going for a drive with the windows down and the music up. But stop bottling it up. It is not healthy, it is not fair and it sure as hell isn't going to solve anything. Get proactive and rid those snarky causing people from your life.

Now, I have dishes to do. Sigh.

MANAGING CHAOS

Give yourself quiet moments in your day. Consciously breathe deeply. Write manageable lists and set realistic goals. Understand that sometimes you can't do everything you want to and that is okay.

This past holiday season was the epitome of chaos. Add working a full time job, dealing with a family, and crazy winter weather, and you have the perfect recipe for exhaustion, overloaded brain circuits and a blood pressure that was off the charts. Chaos. The stores were insane. People pushing and fighting over merchandise, parking spots and food court tables. Elbowing and charging through crowds, like a linebacker in a football game. Forget the real reasons behind the season - everyone was in their own personal nightmare of getting perfect gifts.

The coup de grace to whatever shred of peace you had left - wrapping, cooking, decorating and for some, spending time with relatives they would rather avoid - will surely take care of eradicating any remaining sanity from your world. Chaos reigns and peace slips furtively out the door when you aren't looking.

I found myself in the midst of it the Sunday before Christmas. From the demands of my day job to getting my "To Do" list completed and everything in between - my mind gave in to the chaos. I was exhausted. I was overwhelmed. I had so much to do and so very little time to do it. Throw a Maine ice storm into the mix, and I suddenly felt like a pressure cooker ready to explode.

I had to rein in the chaos and get a hold on my life.

I have been here before and not necessarily just around the holidays. Chaos has a way of creeping in when you least expect it, catching you off guard and taking a sledgehammer to the peace you had been cultivating. Sudden events in one's life can send you reeling. Bills piling up, death of a loved one, ending relationships or the daily struggle of work-life-kids and the day-to-day minutiae that is life. All of it can create a chaos in your mind and in your life that completely over-takes you suddenly and out-of-the-blue one day. Then, like a pressure cooker, you explode. The key is not letting it get to that point. The key is learning to rein the chaos in before it overtakes you and bringing the peace back in. The big thing, get proactive in dealing with the chaos - before the chaos deals with you.

I sat at my kitchen table on this particular day, blood pressure up, heading throbbing, looking around at the chaos inside my home. Realizing it was mimicking the chaos inside my mind and if I didn't get a grip on it, I was going to lose it. I won't lie here, locking myself in my room and hanging a "Do Not Disturb" sign on my door did cross my mind. I wanted to throw my hands in the air and yell, "I QUIT!" Instead, I closed my eyes and wrapped my hands around a steaming mug of coffee. I regulated my breathing. Breathe deeply in through my nose and slowly exhale through my mouth. My focus only on the warmth of my mug and the rhythm of my breath.

In-and-out. In-and-out.

I sat there for about 30 minutes in total silence. Just breathing consciously. As the mug of once hot coffee cooled in my hands, the tightness in my chest eased. When my mind cleared I had a bit of an epiphany. Instead of addressing my feelings of being overwhelmed and taking proactive steps to correct the issues, I had simply allowed it to fester. The ensuing chaos was of my own creation. Not putting my foot down when the signs started showing - allowed the chaos to explode over everything. By not holding others responsible and by being so confident I could do everything on my own, too confident as the case may be, I allowed myself to become overwhelmed. I had closed my eyes and jumped in with both feet. I had to take full responsibility for allowing myself to get to where I was that day.

I also needed to take responsibility for getting myself out of the chaos. That meant stilling my mind and focusing on a game plan for myself. I set attainable goals and numbered them in the order I felt they needed to be accomplished. Some of my goals had deadlines, while others were a bit more open ended. The whole process helped to calm my racing heart and quiet the chaos in my mind.

Give yourself a break once and awhile. Whether it be the holidays or not, chaos can and will find you when you least expect it. It will beat you down and hold you there until you either give up or get proactive in calming it yourself. Give yourself quiet moments in your day. Consciously breathe deeply. Write manageable lists and set realistic goals. Understand that sometimes you can't do everything you want to and that is okay. Do the best you can with what you have and try again tomorrow. Give yourself a deadline on some things and leave others open ended.

Out of chaos - stillness is born.

Stillness of your soul. Stillness of your mind. It has to be this way or one would simply shatter. You must learn to rein in the chaos. You must learn to harness it for use as a stepping stone to get to where you need to be. Chaos to peace. Chaos to order.

Life becoming still once more.
Manageable.

STUCK IN A RUT

The happiest people on the planet are the ones who are constantly trying to better themselves. People who are constantly looking for ways to get better, for ways to improve, to be stronger, smarter and more capable of anything and everything. The happiest and most fulfilled people are the ones who never stop evolving.

Imagine you are driving down a back road through a dense forest, sunshine barely penetrates the full treetops high above you and there is a plume of dust following in your wake. You are not even sure where you are exactly and find you really don't care. You are comfortable and enjoying the moment. As you come around a bend you suddenly see thick storm clouds rolling in over the tall pine trees. You pick up on the metallic smell of rain and the coming storm on the breeze through your window. As you crest a hill, you drive directly into the sudden storm. Rain lashes at your car and what was just a smooth dirt road is now a series of flooded puddles, mud and some serious ruts. Out of nowhere a huge pothole opens up in front of you and having no chance to avoid it, you hit the rut head on. Mud covers the front end of your vehicle and with a sickening feeling you realize you are stuck.

Stuck in a rut.

The storm passes just as quickly as it came. However, you are mired in mud and aren't going anywhere for the time being. You try to dig out your car but it is hard work. You try pushing your car and that too is hard. With the car only giving an inch or less at a time, you grow quickly frustrated. "Why am I not getting anywhere?" you ask yourself, as you pound on the roof. Why me? Why now? Do you just give up? Do you walk until you find help? Do you just sit there in hopes someone finds you?

What do you do when you find yourself stuck in a rut?

Becoming stuck in a rut is not always as in-your-face and can't-miss-it clear as the above scenario, sometimes in life you don't even realize you are so mired in a rut that you can't move. Day in and day out you simply exist. You don't want to try - it's too hard. You don't want to push yourself - it's too much work. You don't want to think, do or plan anything. You don't go out, you don't have fun and you don't do anything except the bare minimum to get through your day. Motivation goes on hiatus, interest in anything goes too. You work, you come home and you veg in front of the television, choosing to "live" the lives of the characters on your favorite sitcoms instead of your own.

Perhaps initially you needed a break from life's chaos. Possibly you suffered a loss, a break-up or life event that you needed to process. Maybe you required some time to acclimate to life changes and in the process of healing your wounds, coming to grip with a new reality, or after making peace with something, you simply forgot to start moving forward again.

Do anything for too long and it becomes a habit.

Hide from the world every chance you get and you will eventually "forget" to get back out there. Set your brain on autopilot and do only the bare minimum to get through the day and this will become your new normal. Lose interest in living life, having fun and making memories and you will find after a while, you cease to care.

Effectively, you cease to care about anything.

If you continue on doing the same thing over and over and over again, you are going to get the same results. Are you happy? Are you satisfied? Or do you feel like you are missing something but have absolutely no idea what it is. It is like driving the exact same route to work every single day. You become oblivious to the scenery because you see it all the time. Then one day you get rerouted because of some construction and are forced to turn down a new road. Immediately your brain kicks on and you start seeing all that is new and different. Maybe you get lucky and find a new coffee shop you never knew existed, maybe you stop at a different convenience store and meet the man of your dreams, who just bought a winning lottery ticket. Things you would have missed out on forever had you never made that turn. Quite frankly, you would have missed out on, because left to your own devices, stuck in your rut, you never would have stepped outside of your comfort zone and done something different in the first place.

The same premise works for life too. But, you have to see the rut you are stuck in first. You have to see it AND want to pull yourself out of it. Maybe you are happy coasting through life. Maybe you think adventure is too scary or happiness is a myth. More likely is the chance you aren't even aware of what you are doing or not doing for that matter and you aren't even aware you are coasting through life and not actually living it at all.

Self-doubting all the time - is a rut. Dating the same type of person that never works out over and over again - is a rut. Working a dead end job beneath your capabilities and not constantly looking for better - is a rut. Allowing fear of what could happen because of what happened in the past to stop you - is a rut. Thinking you don't have to try any longer is one of the biggest ruts of all.

The happiest people on the planet are the ones who are constantly trying to better themselves. People who are constantly looking for ways to get better, for ways to improve, to be stronger, smarter and more capable of anything and everything. Because it makes them feel alive, accomplished and motivated to reach even higher. The happiest and most fulfilled people are the ones who never stop evolving.

Ruts are easy. Ruts hold you tight and at times can feel almost comforting. But ruts hold you back and mire you so deep that happiness no longer exists. Look at your life right now. What can you make better, do better or start doing to fire up that spark of passion and set you on the course of becoming a more fulfilled and happy person? This is what you need to be doing. Not later, not tomorrow, not next week - right now.

Do something that makes you come alive and want to live fully. Explore your passions, your ideas and dig yourself out of whatever rut you find yourself mired in. Find that glimmer of a spark in the center of your soul and do whatever it takes to ignite it. Feed that flame and become alive again. Live in the moment instead of in the rut.

Free yourself!

FAST AND FAST WE GO

We must remember to not get so caught up in making a life, dealing with life or just floating through life that we actually forget to live life. Stop chasing happiness, stop chasing that pot of gold and stop chasing those better tomorrows. Those better tomorrows are right now, because right now is all we have.

I remember sitting on the cold steel disk with my back up against the cylinder at its center, holding on to the posts and watching as the trees, buildings and people, all began to blur together. Faster and faster I would spin in circles. At first keeping my eyes wide open, watching everything blend together, then after a moment, I would close them and imagine I was spinning through time and when I stopped, I would have been magically transported to another world. As I felt the disk start to slow I would gather all my strength to greet my new beginning and every time would be sadden to realize I was still in the same place, the local playground on the merry-go-round, surrounded by shrieking and laughing kids. No new world, no magical forests with unicorns and fairies, just my existing life. Always convincing myself that maybe I hadn't believed enough or wasn't spinning fast enough - that next time it would work. I think I was eight years old.

As I grow older I find myself thinking back to those merry-go-rounds, realizing that in a way, they really are a symbol of life and time. So fast do the days blur together, weeks seem to disappear in a heartbeat and before we know what happened, years have come and gone.

Yet, we continue to spin on to some future time when things will be better, we will be happier; we will be ready to live.

Sometimes, like on the merry-go-round, life appears to be spinning out of our control, so we hang on as tight as we can, fear of letting go and crashing down weighting us to one spot. We close our eyes against the blur of time rushing past and hope against hope when we open them everything will have changed for the better. Or we sit there with our backs up against the center, as the world spins around us, uncertainty filling our souls. Do we risk letting go? Do we risk the uncertainty of where we will land if we take the chance of throwing up our arms and leaping? Safe landings are never guaranteed - what happens if we take the chance and get hurt? Will we get back up and if we do, will we have the courage to try again?

I also think back to the times when I was on the merry-go-round and the trust I had to place in the person who was controlling the speed. Knowing it was completely out of my control and always thinking I needed to speak up for myself, needed to tell them I wasn't okay with what they were doing, that I was frightened and scared of getting hurt. I remember feeling trapped between the posts, my back up against the center and feeling whatever happened next was not something I could do anything about. I just had to hold on and hope for the best. Reminds me of a good portion of my life. Where the needs of others always came first and I was left with my back against the wall wondering when it would be my turn to control my life.

I remember once spinning so fast I thought for sure it was going to fly off its post - the world became a single blurred image and I became scared. I felt my hands suddenly let go of the posts and the next thing I remember is lying on the ground wondering what had happened. I was stunned, I was terrified and I couldn't take a breath. I remember thinking I would never be able to get back up on my feet. Reminds me of those times in life when the world seemed to crashing all around me. When it had knocked me to my knees and took the breath out of me. Times when it took every ounce of courage I had to get back up again. How easy it would have been to just sit there and play it safe. Just like those moments in your life when something broke your spirit, your heart and shattered your soul. We must always find the courage to pick ourselves up, catch our breath and begin again. Life is too precious to waste and giving up should never been an option.

Life is always going to spin. At times it may start to feel like that merry-go-round at the playground, faster and faster and out of your control. There will be blurred times, dark times, light filled times and stretches of crazy out-of-control times. And while we can't control the passage of time, we can control how we spend it. In fact, it is something we must do. We must consciously be aware of the moments we have, the fears that hold us back and that sometimes we just have to let go and allow ourselves the freedom to fly.

We must remember to not get so caught up in making a life, dealing with life or just floating through life that we actually forget to live life. Stop chasing happiness, stop chasing that pot of gold and stop chasing those better tomorrows. Those better tomorrows are right now, because right now is all we have. Cherish it.

QUEEN OF DENIAL

We can't let go of something if we have a strangle hold on it in the first place. Whether you realize it or not, you are holding on to everything you never deal with. Just because you have buried it so far down into the depths of your soul, doesn't mean it won't ever come back up. It just means you really good at burying things.

Just because you refuse to see something, doesn't mean it isn't there. Just because you refuse to think about something, doesn't mean it no longer requires thought. Just because you refuse to deal with something, doesn't make it disappear.

Just because you convince yourself that you are okay, doesn't mean you actually are.

Growing up as the daughter of a severely bipolar mother, I began to understand the importance of stark in-your-face reality. My mother lived in a world of "created reality," meaning she created what she wanted. She saw what she wanted. She heard what she wanted. She remembered as she wanted. She would make one question everything they held to be true, because she was so convincing and believable. As a teenager I seriously thought more often than not that I was losing my mind. I would remember something one way and she would remember it happening in a completely different way. She would fight and argue with you until you either started second guessing yourself or just gave in.

She also was the queen of denial. If she did not want to see something, deal with something or make a decision - she simply didn't. Rest of the world be damned.

As I grew up I started to understand more the importance of facing reality head on. Never allowing it to blur. Never turning my back on it and hoping it would go away. Good, bad or indifferent, I needed to see it for what it was. Believe in it, deal with it and then make peace with it and move on. I had to grow to trust myself and my perceptions. Which growing up the way I did is often easier said than done. I began to figure out that if something needed facing - then I needed to face it. If something needed to be dealt with - then I needed to deal with it. If a decision needed to be made, regardless of how hard it was - then I needed to make it. Right then and there. It might have taken me months to work through something, but I had to actively work on it. Not pretend it wasn't there, hadn't happened or would get better if I just ignored it. I had to deal with whatever it was and then let it go.

Reality.

One of my best friends suffered a tremendous loss last year. She really had no idea how to handle what had happened. So she didn't. She packed up, moved on and refused to talk about it. If you were to ask her how she was doing, she would reply just fine and then change the subject. Her sleep became erratic. She began having nightmares. She would either lose her appetite completely or binge-eat for hours. She would drink herself into a stupor every night and always her reply would be the same - I'm fine. Except she wasn't. Not even close. But because she refused to face the reality that she was hurting and to do something about it, she continued to spiral down.

One day recently she, without thinking, stopped at a coffee shop she used to visit regularly with the person she lost. She hadn't been back there since he died and it was the mundane act of ordering coffee that broke through to her. She sat in her car as reality crashed all around her. Crying, she faced the fact she wasn't fine. That she had simply buried her pain and had done herself more harm than she would have, had she faced it to begin with. She has begun the road to healing now and is taking her life back.

Another friend of mine has a husband who is an alcoholic. Everyone sees it. Most have had to experience his drunken behavior at one time or another. Friends have stopped visiting their house. They do not get invited to parties or out to dinner any more. His fits of rage and theatrics are known to all by now, and while they love and adore her, they just can't take him anymore. When he is not drinking he is an amazingly funny and generous guy, but that guy doesn't show up much. A few of her close friends have tried to sit her down to talk about it. She just makes excuses for him and changes the subject. She refuses to see that there is a problem and regardless of how much love and support we can give her, we can't force her to see something she doesn't want to.

Just because you ignore something does not in fact make it go away. It means this 'something' is sitting there, waiting to jump out and catch you unaware. You may be traveling along the road of your life, all happy and at peace (or so you convince yourself) when out-of-the-blue you see something, read something or hear something that triggers a cascade of memories and emotions you should have dealt with long ago. It literally can drive you to your knees and feel like your heart is breaking all over again. Thing of it is, your heart never healed in the first place. Not if you refused to face what happened. If you never dealt with the past, refuse to see the current situation or handled a life event head-on, your heart is still in pieces. Because in order to be whole once more, you have to come to terms with whatever it is that happened or that is happening now. Otherwise you have just put a Band-Aid on your heart and your soul hoping that it holds the broken pieces together.

The truth of it is - it may hold, for a while... but it won't hold forever.

Recently an older lady reached out to me concerning a passage in my book. The piece I had written had apparently gone through every level of defense she had created over the past 30-something years and hit straight to the core of a childhood she never made peace with. We talked at length about the struggles life can bring to us, and about not dealing with things that had happened. We talked about how not coming to some sort of real peace with it once and for all, can color everything we do going forward. We don't trust others, we don't trust ourselves. We develop addictions, or coping mechanisms that do nothing to actually make it better.

We can't let go of something if we have a strangle hold on it in the first place. Whether you realize it or not, you are holding on to everything you never deal with. Just because you have buried it so far down into the depths of your soul, doesn't mean it won't ever come back up. It just means you are really good at burying things. Believe me, you may not consciously realize the affect everything you haven't dealt with, made peace with or see for what it really is, has on your life. Step back for a moment and take a hard look at yourself. The walls you have built up, the stories you tell yourself, the things you avoid so that you don't trigger painful memories. What triggers your anger, your hurt and your sadness? Do you see a pattern here?

The brilliant thing is, when you make the decision to bring all the bad and all the dark out into the light so that you can deal with once and for all - You are in total control. Remind yourself that it is over, it can't hurt you anymore. Find ways to confront things head-on and understand that if you continue to ignore or bury whatever it is that needs to be released, you effectively give away all of your power.

You are strong enough to face it.

Trust in yourself to see your way through. I won't promise you it will be easy. I will promise you it will be worth it.

WHEN YOU WISH UPON A STAR

"When you wish upon a star, makes no difference who you are. Anything your heart desires will come to you. If your heart is in your dreams, no request is too extreme...."
~Jiminy Cricket

You find yourself outside on a clear night, the stars are shining brightly and the moon a brilliant giant orb that seems to pull at your soul. You are contemplative and dreamy, bedtime is fast approaching and your defenses are down. Your mind is wandering and for this stolen moment you are at peace. Suddenly, a flash of white streaks the night sky - shooting star. You close your eyes and make a wish...

What do you wish for?

Recently I asked my followers on the Random Thoughts Facebook page a similar question. The altruistic responses aside, I was more interested in what people wished for themselves. While a few declined to share for fear their wishes wouldn't come true, a lot answered. People responded they would wish for new jobs, new homes, more money, health and someone even wished for their 20-year-old body back. Wishes really ran the gamut but a lot of them were practical and attainable. Someone asked me what I would wish for and the first thing that popped into my mind was my wish to be able to write full-time. Attainable, yes, if I work hard enough and sell enough books. But as I went about my day I took the question and mulled it over.

What would I wish for?

I kept coming back to the same thing over and over again. Recognizing as the day went on that apparently this "wish" was something that had been on my mind without me even realizing the importance. I wished for no drama, no stress and more time. Three things that seem to occupy my world whether I want them there or not. I want peace. I want people to behave as they should, do as they should and I want time enough to do everything I need to do, like spend time with my husband.

It dawned on me as I was contemplating time, drama and stress that I could actually control two out of the three. I will never be able to control time - I have tried. You can't get it back once it is gone, you can't bank some to use later and regardless of how hard I wish, I simply cannot add more hours to the day. I get 24-hours just like everyone else. But what I can control is how I use those 24-hours.

This leads me to the other two.

Drama. I hate it. Can't stand it. Have no place for it, no time for it and no inclination to deal with it. But deal with it I must for there are some people who bring it into my world whether I want it or not. Do I actually have to deal with other people's drama? It can be so easy to get caught up in it, play into it and become embroiled in it before even realizing what is happening. That is not their fault, these drama queens. It is totally mine. Because I allowed it to enter my world. I entertained it and know what, I didn't have to. I could shut them down, tune them out or politely decline to deal with it. I could walk away, ignore it or if it directly affected me put my foot down and stop it. We control what we allow into our lives. We control. If you have someone in your life who is constantly picking fights, gossiping about others, starting battles or generally living like their life is a soap opera - stop entertaining them. Control your life and the cast of characters in it. Their temper tantrums, their need for chaos or need to wind up everyone is of no concern to you, unless you allow it. Stop allowing it.

A freeing thought isn't it?

Stress. Aside from everyday stress, which unfortunately is life, the stress certain people bring into your life all the time is, for lack of a more eloquent phrase, a pain in the ass. It is hard enough when it is friends or co-workers, even more difficult when it is family and you are obligated to deal with them. Or are you? Like the drama queens who start problems, there are those people who behave in a way that without fail will cause you intense stress. Emotional vampires who suck the contentment out of your life and replace it with a riled up stomach, knotted muscles, racing heart and - if you are like me - a headache. People who do not respect you, take advantage of you or back you into corners, pile insults on you or use you every chance they get. You know how they are. You know who they are. You allow yourself to become entangled with them over and over because you simply think you have to.

Guess what! You don't.

People who cause you stress all the time, who disrespect you or take advantage of you - do not deserve any time in your life. Stop allowing them room in your mind. The only people who should be in your world are the ones YOU want there. People who treat you with the respect you deserve, who love you and people who believe in you. You are always going to have assholes to deal with in life, that is a given, but deal with them and be done with it. Stop letting them back into your life again and again. Control your happiness. Control your world. If someone needs to go, but won't on their own, then stand up for yourself and leave them. You don't have to make a big deal out of it. You don't have to make a scene, leave that for the drama queen but make a conscious decision on who has a place in your life. Stop entertaining those who don't.

I have, over the years, weeded out some people who over and over again hurt me, lied to me, used me or basically brought so much drama into my life that it affected me mentally. Each time they would flare up I would swear to myself it would be the last time, only for a long time, it wasn't. I would allow them back again and again because I felt like I had to. But then one day I made a few wishes. Attainable wishes for sure. I wished for peace, I wished for contentment and I wished to be happy. Then I wished a big one. One that for me was harder to attain, but one that eventually did come true. I wished I would realize I was worth my wishes coming true. My wishes for happiness, peace and contentment were worth fighting for because I deserved them. But, and this is a big BUT, I had to make them come true - by believing in me.

Same thing goes for you. You deserve to be happy, peaceful and content. Make your wish and then believe in yourself enough to make them all come true.

I think Jiminy Cricket sang it best...."*When you wish upon a star, makes no difference who you are. Anything your heart desires will come to you. If your heart is in your dreams, no request is too extreme....*"

Make your wish.

FOOL ME ONCE

Trust yourself enough to know your instincts, your reactions and the tingling on the back of your neck will rarely lead you wrong.

I did something recently that I almost never do. Something so totally unlike me that looking back over the situation really makes me shake my head and feel like a fool. It is not a feeling I like. It is not one I am accustomed to, either. I am a lot of things but a fool normally isn't one of them. Well, except for maybe this time and okay maybe a few other times over the years, but I do not normally allow myself to be made a fool of. Especially when I did the one thing I know better than to do.

I ignored my gut feeling.

I also ignored what I have dubbed my "Spidey Sense" - that tingling at the back of your neck when you know something isn't right, someone isn't being truthful or maybe you have stepped into an unsafe environment and though you can't see the threat, you can feel it. I always, ALWAYS, listen to my gut. I always pay attention to my Spidey Sense and rarely am I bamboozled by someone. It happens, I know that. But normally not to me. I always trust my instincts and I am normally right. Except of course when I disregard them. Which I did. Which looking back on is all sorts of a rookie mistake that I should know better than to make.

But make it I did.

Apparently the universe decided I needed a life lesson, a reminder if you will, to trust my instincts and stop ignoring something just because I don't want to see it. The only positive thing to come out of the whole mess was it got me thinking. About all the times in my life someone has spoken the words - "I knew it the whole time, but didn't want to see it," or " In my gut I knew something was wrong, but I ignored it, now I am picking up the pieces." Or, and this is a big one, "I should have trusted my instincts."

Which translates into - I should have trusted myself.

How many of you honestly trust yourselves? Do you trust your own judgment; trust your reactions, your gut instincts and your own version of the Spidey Sense? Or do you find you are constantly second guessing yourself, listening more to what others are telling you and trusting in their judgment more than you trust in yourself to be right? It is a question that requires a bit of soul searching and willingness to take a hard look within.

The thing of it is, if something gets your gut instincts fired up, your Spidey Sense tingling and you refuse to see, won't allow yourself to see or pretend not to see the red flags or the cause of what is triggering it all, for whatever reason, you are then responsible in part for what happens next. This was the case with me this past week. I chose to ignore certain comments that were said, look past behaviors that were a clear indication of the type of person I was dealing with, all because I wanted so much to believe in him. I wanted to help this person with his business because he helped people in a way that inspired me. I wanted to believe in him, so I ignored the warning signs and ignored what my gut was telling me. I allowed him to bamboozle me. I chose not to see things for what they were, and it cost me a lot of time, money and peace of mind.

How many times in your life have you done this same thing? Maybe facing the truth was too hard, too much to bear. Maybe you didn't want to handle the fallout or felt you weren't strong enough to face it. You silence your instincts, turn a blind eye and pretend all is what you want it to be.

Stop.

By not listening to your gut instincts, not heeding the Spidey Sense and not seeing things for what they really are, you are selling yourself and your life short. Who wants to live a lie? Or live with the fear that some day will come when you can't avoid the truth any longer, can't avoid seeing things for what they really are and all of a sudden, BOOM! It's in your face whether you are ready or not.

Trust yourself enough to know your instincts, your reactions and the tingling on the back of your neck will rarely lead you wrong. I don't care if it is among strangers, out shopping with the girls or a chance meeting with a new potential date. I don't care if it happens with someone you have been close to, married to or dating for years. I don't care if it is your child, your neighbor, or some salesman at the door - trust your instincts. Value your judgment and listen to YOURSELF! Stop turning a blind eye and start seeing things for how they actually are and not how you really wish they were. It may hurt, your heart may break, you may feel like a fool but at least you listened to yourself. It will surprise you how much heartache and misery you will avoid in life once you start trusting your instincts.

Follow your gut.

SQUARE PEG ROUND HOLE

I shall write a letter. I will address it to my younger self, because when you boil it down - the basic principles of life haven't changed. Everyone wants to matter. Everyone wants to fit in. From the children of today to the children of yesterday who still live inside each and every one of us.

Have you ever tried to fit a square peg into a round hole? Figured out pretty quick that no matter how hard you push, turn and threaten - it just won't fit? Welcome to my world. I am the square peg and the world, well; the world is a big round hole I will never force myself to fit into. There are a lot of us you know - though not all are square. A plethora of different shapes and not a single one of them will ever fit into that perfectly round hole. Though, I think there are many who wish they could.

You can't force something to fit in when it was born to stand out.

Well, at least this is what I tell myself every day when reality rears its head and again shows me just how different I am from others. I celebrate this now. I didn't always. Especially through parts of my scholastic career - mainly middle and high school. Though I can say, looking back now, I feel proud of the way I handled those tumultuous times. I didn't realize then how much I was shaping my world of today - not by anything I actually studied in books - but what I learned from handling situations that should have put me into therapy for years. The lesson that took me 17 years to fully appreciate.

It is a lesson I wish I could travel to every single school and announce loudly over the PA system or better yet into the ear-buds of every single school-age child. It is a lesson with many facets. Intricate, yet simple. So, seeing that I can't figure out a way to take-over all the ear-buds in the world, I shall write a letter. I will address it to my younger self, because when you boil it down - the basic principles of life haven't changed. Everyone wants to matter. Everyone wants to fit in. From the children of today to the children of yesterday who still live inside each and every one of us.

A lesson I wish someone had told me back then.

Dear *Younger Self,*

I saw you walking home from the bus stop after school with downcast eyes and sagging shoulders. They teased you again today. Though you held your head up at the time, refusing to show the pain their words inflicted, I know you were breaking inside. I know you were taking their taunts and weaving them into your own, which always run on repeat inside your head.

I saw you this morning looking into the mirror, echoes of the insults and comments ringing in your mind. The tears you refuse to shed now glistening in your eyes, as you see yourself, not as you really are, but as they say you are - in your reflection. Still you repeat the words over and over again. Knowing they must be true. You begin to torment yourself, harsher words than even the kids at school said. They can't hurt you any worse than you hurt yourself every single day.

Stop staring into that mirror and only seeing what they say is there. Just stop. Look into the mirror and see the fierceness in your eyes - that spark. For it is that spark they are afraid of. The spark money can't buy. They fear it and will do their damnedest to blow it out. You must never let that happen.

Younger Self, though no one will confirm it, well some may try to but you won't believe them, you do in fact matter. Even if right now you feel as if you have no say, no control or no power, you do. In fact, you have more than most. You must understand this first piece of knowledge I hand down to you - you do matter. A lot. You matter to the most important person in the whole world - You matter to you. I know the words and actions of others hurt. I know no one supports you. Not at home and not out in the world. I know you feel you are on your own and in reality - you are. Instead of being ashamed of that, see how strong it makes you. I know all you want to do is fit in. But, you never will. You were never supposed to. You are supposed to stand out.

Understand Younger Self, people in this world fear things that are different. They will try to destroy things they perceive as better, smarter or prettier than they are. They will shatter things they cannot understand or comprehend. Because to them it highlights their weaknesses. They will try to break you down - You must NEVER allow it. You must never resort to violence to solve things. Learn to defend yourself, yes - but never instigate or hurt another person if you can help it. Your words and your intelligence are your weapon of choice. Use them in all situations if possible. You must stand firm - even when you are shaking inside. This will get easier as time goes on. I promise.

Always stand your ground against people who mock you, question you and always meet their gaze. Never drop your eyes to the floor again. It is not in you to play small. Even when you do not feel confident. Even as they tease and torment you. Look them square in the eye and refuse to break. Do not give their words any weight. Do not give their words any power, for they are not YOUR words. Your words, your thoughts - are what matter.

Over and over you must do this. You must always live by the code you set for yourself. Your principles, ethics, behavior and character are what will define you in life. Not your home-life, clothing, hair or body. Trust in that. The world may define a person by the clothes they wear - but you must never accept that. You are going to make mistakes. Mistakes are awesome – because they are one step closer to getting it right. Learn from your mistakes. Own them and move on from them. Some you may make a couple of times before you get it right. This is okay. This is how you learn. You must never fail to see the lesson. Lessons from your mistakes will make you a better person.

I will not lie to you and tell you living this way is easy - it isn't. I will not tell you that loneliness will not consume you at times - it will. I will not tell you that it gets better when you are older either. There will be times when you wonder if life would be easier if you just followed the crowd. Your strength however will be gained in building your road in life. You are smart enough. You are capable. You can handle anything life throws at you. Trust in this.

Younger Self, you have a voice. Learn early on to use it. Do not remain silent when you see another being hurt. Always protect those who cannot protect themselves. Use your voice for others who cannot find their own. Never stand idle when others are being taunted - just because it isn't you, does not mean you tolerate it. Doesn't matter if it is not the cool thing to do. Doesn't matter if the "in-crowd" doesn't approve. You must use that fire inside of your soul for others. Be brave.

Young One, learn to be friends with anyone, just as long as they are good. Do not listen just to the words coming out of their mouth - study their actions as well. Look beyond the bravado and see what is in their eyes. People will lie to you. People will spread rumors and gossip. Some will try to discredit you. Learn to let it go. Learn to trust that your work, character and integrity will always shine through. Those who choose to believe the lies do not deserve a place in your life - let them go. Learn the lesson this teaches you and use it going forward through life.

Learn to deal with the bullies. Learn to control your fear and use your intelligence. Bullies do not disappear when you graduate, there are many out in the real world too. Learn to stand your ground. Learn to never dull your shine. For every one person who doesn't like you there will be dozens who do. Trust me on that.

The world will constantly try and get you to sell out. To conform. People will try and change you to fit into the acceptable mold. Never let anyone define who you are. Define yourself. It is a rough road to follow but trust in your later years you will have built the character and confidence to see yourself through anything. You must keep going. Always keep going. The world needs you.

I need you.

Though you may feel alone and like the world would be better off without you in it - it will not always be like this. You have the power to create a *world you want. Fill it with friends who love you. There will be dark days for sure, but that spark you never allowed to go out - will always burn brightly helping you to find your way.*

Trust you will always find your way. Believe in your power. Believe in better days. Believe in yourself. Doesn't matter if the world doesn't seem to. Doesn't matter what others say. There are more out there just like you. Promise.

Trust in your journey. It's worth it.

Love,
Your Future Self

WEIGHT OF THE WORLD

I am scared to shrug my shoulders see, for the weight of the world rests there and I am afraid of causing another catastrophe.

Do you ever feel like you are carrying the weight of the world on your shoulders and that one wrong move will tip the balancing act, causing it to all come crashing down? Do you sometimes wish you could set the burden down and rest a bit or let someone else carry it for a while? Do you continue on each and every day hoping that with each step your load will lessen some? Yeah, me too.

In reality though, it never really seems to. In fact, more and more seems to get added to it until you're not sure if you can even stand, let alone walk with it any more. But, somehow you do and you find the strength you need, from some part of you that even you didn't know existed. It amazes me the strength one can find when they dig deeper into their soul. Even when exhaustion, stress and the burdens of life make it feel impossible to continue on. But continue on you do. Day in and day out. What other option is there really? Give up? Not in my world.

Life can be exhausting. Stress builds up. More responsibilities are added to your already sagging shoulders. Things do not go as planned. Something breaks. Someone gets sick. So many things seem to come at once and we are forced to shoulder it. Shoulder it, work through it and try not to collapse. Sometimes our load gets so heavy and without an end in sight, feels like it will crush us before the day is done. Thinking to ourselves that at some point, enough has to be enough. Right? There has to be a stretch of time where everything magically goes right. A moment when everything fits into place and the world revolves without us having to do anything.

As I sit here writing this in a few stolen moments in my day, I sigh. Just the thought of a stretch of time, with no stress or drama, nothing to handle, deal with or get through - makes me smile. Well smile and shake my head knowing a day dream when I see it. Or maybe not. Maybe there is a way, to once in a while set your load down, catch your breath and just be. A way to get life to leave you alone for a while. Allowing you to decompress and put your own head and thoughts in order. If you allow yourself to be drained, emotionally exhausted and stressed to the max all the time, and you keep putting aside your need for a break day-after-day to handle everything for everyone else, you will eventually collapse. Do it for months on end, even years, until that one day suddenly arrives when you just can't shoulder the load anymore and you know what will happen? You will begin to resent everything and everyone. You will feel taken advantage of, burdened and hopeless. Don't focus on your needs occasionally, and no one but you will suffer the consequences.

You have to put it down for a while or else it will crush you. Setting down your burdens, releasing your stress for a moment is not a sign of weakness. It is the epitome of true strength.

We all have to realize we are human.

We cannot be expected to handle everything all of the time without some break. We have to learn and teach ourselves to set the load down once and a while. Allowing us time to turn our attention inward and focus on our needs. We have to hold our hand up and say stop. Stop the drama. Stop the stress. Stop going around in circles. Life is too short. If we don't look up once in a while - we will miss it. We will miss it while we are fixing everything and anything but ourselves.

I swear I can hear some of you right now, sighing and saying to yourself – never going to happen. Just not possible. There are things to do. Kids to feed. A sick loved one who needs care. Bills to be paid. Houses to clean. Work to get to. If I stop and take some time for myself – the world will end. So what if I am exhausted? So what if I am unhappy? Just because I am stressed, doesn't give me license to be selfish. I have responsibilities. Things I have no choice but to take on and place on my shoulders with everything else. No one else will do it. No one ever does. It is all up to me.

Stop being a damn martyr.

I want you, right now, to do something. I want you to honestly examine all the stress, responsibilities and "life" you have currently piled on your shoulders. Really look at it. Take the blinders off and actually see it all clearly. Now, answer me this... How much of this is actually your burden? How much of it belongs to someone else who should be the one taking care of it?

The older I get the more I realize - I tend to pick up a lot that is not mine. Be it at home, work or when it comes to family and friends. I will see something that needs doing, handling or figuring out and not see anyone claiming it. So I do. I think it's because growing up everything was always my responsibility. Well, in hindsight it really wasn't, but that is what I was conditioned to accept. Everyone else's happiness was on me. If that meant taking care of things they should have been taking care of, then that is what I did. So much so, I have incorporated it into my adult self without even realizing. Instead of leaving things that were never mine to begin with alone, I pick it up. Instead of refusing to do things that someone else should be doing – I do it. I add it to the growing pile on my shoulders, even when I am almost to my knees by the sheer weight of my burdens.

I have learned, though, a few lessons over the past couple of years.

The first lesson – The world will not end if I take a mental health day. A day where the only thing I focus on is, me. Okay, maybe not a whole day but at least part of a day.

The second lesson – Breaking down the burden into manageable bits helps tremendously. I can multi task with the best of them but in doing so, overwhelm myself more often than not. So, I tackle the bigger things one at a time. If it is something I can take care of and be done with it, I do. If it is something that requires more attention, I give it the attention is requires and then be done with it.

The third lesson – Holding others accountable for things they should be dealing with. You can't expect someone to face something, deal with something or accept responsibility for something if you are always taking care of it for them. Allow them to be responsible. And understand that it is their choice to do it or not. Not yours. Let it go.

The fourth lesson – Finish each day and be done with it. Set it down and know that you did your best for the day. Give yourself a break. Release it for the night. Light a candle and pretend all of your burdens live in the flame. Say your piece for what happened today – then blow the candle out. You can rekindle your flame and pick it all back up tomorrow. But for the night time – let it go.

I wish for you strength to continue on and the knowledge that while it is hard now, over time you will lose that weight on your shoulders and be free. Just remember, you are strong enough, smart enough and tough enough. And know that setting your load down for a while, to catch your breath, is not weakness. It is a sign you value yourself enough to rest for a while. It is a sign of true strength. The world will not shift off its axis, the sky will not come falling down, I promise. It will all be there to pick back up when you are ready, but, only when you are ready. One foot in front of the other. One day at a time. Pieces will eventually fall into place and your hard work; your perseverance will pay off. You will be free and you will be ready to take on the world.

Deep breath. You got this.

WE ARE ALL CONNECTED

*Take people for who they are. Take people on how they treat those who
can do nothing for them. Take people for the quality of their heart
and soul. These are the true measures of the human race.
You don't have to agree with them to make it so.
You just have to release the need to prove them wrong.*

Several years ago a friend and I were sitting on the sidelines of my step-son's soccer game. Watching the little kids run up and down the field, while family and friends cheered them on, was one of my favorite things to do. As the game came to an end and we were making our way across the field to the parking lot, a young child about six or so was walking with his father just in front of us. The little boy kept stealing glances back at my friend, when out-of-the-blue the child pulled on his father's hand and said in a matter of fact tone; "Daddy, look at the woman, she is so fat." The father, glancing back said to his son; "She sure is kiddo."

I was horrified. Even more so when the father went on to tell his son people who are fat were lazy and shouldn't be out in public. I looked over to my friend and was thankful to see her so engrossed in conversation with my nephew, she hadn't heard the exchange. I was furious. I looked at this father and son walking across the field, right-as-rain, and thought to myself, lazy? This coming from a man who I knew drank his lunch most days, hadn't worked in more than three years and lived off unemployment and state aid for no other reason than he didn't want to look for work. He was calling my friend lazy?

Another friend of mine is a single dad. Recently, he took his five-year-old daughter to a park not far from their home. As he was sitting on the bench watching his little girl laugh with delight each time she went down the slide, he noticed a group of women staring at him. Before long, two of them marched over to him and demanded to know what he was doing starring at the little children and proclaimed they were going to call the police. What was a lone man doing at a playground? Calling him a pervert loud enough for the kids to hear as they strode away. He quickly collected his daughter and left.

I overheard parts of a conversation a table full of teenagers were having the other day while out to lunch. They were discussing ways they could help a newcomer to their school acclimate and make friends. They appeared angry at the reception she had received so far and even the teachers were not all that inclined to get involved. One girl piped up she would do whatever was needed but they couldn't do it at her home because her parents would never approve of her being friends with a foreigner, especially one who was still learning English. She went on to say to her friends that she didn't care what her parents believed, she was going to be friends with the new girl, but thought it best not to let them know.

There is not one person in this entire universe who is perfect. Each and every one of us has flaws. Visible and invisible flaws that we are, for the most part, well aware of. Skinny people are told to eat more. Overweight people are lazy and told to exercise. Beautiful people are dumb and unattractive people are revered for their intelligence. People who swear are horrible and people who worship differently are going to hell. Men can only love women and women can only love men. Men are the breadwinners and are noted for their prowess and take charge attitudes. Women doing the same are labeled "bitch" and horrible mothers because they chose to work, too. The old are no longer viable in the workplace, yet the young are incapable as well and lack the experience to do things right. People from foreign lands are looked at with disdain and fear. Religions battle each other over whose god is the right god and who has the keys to heaven.

Blood is shed, lives are ruined and entire generations are affected. All because people fear that which is different, that which they do not understand and that which goes against their personal belief systems. People live and die by their perceptions.

Perception.

People are not seen as they are. People are seen as we are. Our perceptions, our history and our very being determine what we see and how we react to each and every person we see, meet and interact with. People should not have to be "tolerated" for being different than us, tolerated means they are somehow wrong, inferior or lower than we are. Just because someone worships differently or not at all - does NOT in fact make them a horrible person. It makes them different from you. Just because someone worships in a church, synagogue or temple - does in fact NOT make them wrong. It just makes them different from you. People from other parts of the world are not all terrorists. Women do not have to have children. Men can cry at movies and still be manly.

Different is not wrong. It is just different. There are some people in the world who need to just accept that. Live and let live and focus on themselves, their lives and their families and worry less about what others are doing.

We are different from one another in big ways, small ways and in the nuances that make us who we are. I honestly have thought long and hard about the narrow-mindedness I see every single day.

I asked my followers on the Random Thought's Facebook page the following question to see what their thoughts were; "We live in a world filled with diversity. Why do you think then, people are completely intolerant of others who are not just like them? What can we do to make this better?" I regret my choice of the word intolerant. I will not tolerate certain actions. I will not tolerate certain behaviors in my life. Tolerating is a personal level of comfort to what one will and will not accept in one's life. A better choice of word would have been - release. Why can't we release the notion that people need to be just like us to be good? Why can't we release old outdated notions that have no basis in today's culture? Why can't we release our fear and just accept the fact not everyone is like us? They don't have to be. This is one of the greatest things about living on this planet. We are all different. It makes life interesting. Celebrate differences. Don't hate them. I was astounded with the depth of some of their answers. All but a few echoed my sentiments exactly – we need to release our need to be right and the need for others who are different or think different to be wrong.

I do not care what you do for a living. I do not care if you own a home, rent a studio or live in a commune. I do not care how much money you make, what kind of car you drive or even which football team you cheer for. I do not care how much education you have or what position you hold at your job. I do not care if you are tall and skinny, short and skinny or round and jolly. I do not care how you worship, if you worship or when you worship. I do not care if you are old or young. I do not care about the color of your skin, your choice of partner or whether you eat meat or not. I do not care simply because none of these things determine your worth as a human being in my eyes.

Yes, there are evil men in this world but you cannot judge an entire gender on them. Yes, there are beautiful people in this world who are ignorant, there are just as many less attractive ones who are too. Yes, there are women getting married to other women and no that does not in fact jeopardize the entire human race. Yes, some fat people are lazy and some skinny people do have eating disorders but to judge every single thin or overweight person by these measures is ridiculous. The time to release all preconceived notions of how people are strictly based on our perceptions of them, and the accepted stereotypes, is now.

Release the need for everyone in this world to be just like you. Understand the actions of one, do not dictate the actions of all. Take people for who they are. Take people on how they treat those who can do nothing for them. Take people for the quality of their heart and soul. These are the true measures of the human race.

You don't have to agree with them to make it so.
You just have to release the need to prove them wrong.

NOTHING BUT THE TRUTH

Live honestly with yourself. You have to trust yourself and accept nothing less from the people in your life. Remember some people will tell you what you want to hear so they can feel better. Trust in the ones who tell you what you need to hear so that you can get better.

Tell the truth, the whole truth, and nothing but the truth. But what if your truth and my truth are completely different? What if my perception of the truth is a complete opposite of yours? What if something I live by, hold close to my heart and swear by, is something that rings false in your eyes, in your heart and in your mind?

What then?

Well, then we must learn a very simple but yet complex lesson. There are personal truths, there are black and white truths and there are life altering truths. Truth is relative to the situation in which we find ourselves. Not every truth has an opposing falsehood. Some truths are simply that - true.

Belief systems are personal truths. What I believe to be truth IS truth - for me. You may believe something completely opposite from me and you are neither right nor wrong and neither am I. What we are is right for ourselves. I have absolutely no right to tell you that your truths are wrong. No right to look you in the eye and say that your truth and your beliefs are invalid because they are not mine. Nor do you have the right to say that to me.

Then there are black and white truths. Meaning, for example, if I look outside and see that it is snowing and someone else looks outside and says it is sunny and in the high 80s, one of us is telling a lie. Black and white truths are the most destructive of all. For it is from these truths that lies are born. Black and white truths are not subject to perception, not subject to one's beliefs and are the truths that get twisted, turned, and reworked the most.

Lies get spun for a myriad of reasons to be sure, but wrong nonetheless.

Often the black and white truths can lead to life altering truths, more so when they have been covered up by lies and falsehoods for a period of time. The truth can set you free in a more literal sense.

Once upon a time before I was born, a lie was conceived to cover a truth about who my father really was. Years later when the truth eventually came to light, as it always seems to, life was completely altered for me. A friend of mine is also facing a life-altering truth when he found out his wife of 15 years has been having an affair. Black and white truths are subject to manipulation, to cover-ups and for all the wrong reasons. Usually to save someone else problems, heartache or keep themselves from getting into trouble.

I have zero tolerance for liars.

People who take the truth and twist it or completely discard it and recreate something new in its place, are one of my biggest pet peeves in life. Someone who tells a new story or new "truth" that is completely based on lies, in order to get something they do not deserve, avoid something that they shouldn't or to hide transgressions that they have done, make me furious. Then there are those people who tell lies about others in order to discredit them, or to make the liar appear to be someone they are not. There is a woman I know who is constantly manipulating the truth so as to make herself appear to be a better person than she really is, usually telling lies about others in order to make herself look good. It drives me absolutely insane. Instead of trying to better herself, she focuses all of her attention creating a new "reality," that anyone who spends even the smallest amount of time poking holes in the smokes screens, could see through. I think though, she has done this for so long that she has actually started to believe in a lot of the lies.

This leads me to my next thought, the lies we tell ourselves.

It is bad enough when someone we love and trust, lie to us. But what is even worse is when we lie to ourselves. Big or little lies, it doesn't matter, it is destructive and such a huge waste of time. Time we could be using to correct something, face something, and deal with something, instead of lying to ourselves because we aren't strong enough to face the truth. I think one of the biggest lies we tell ourselves on a daily basis is; "I'm fine" when in fact we are anything but.

Kind of a fake it til you make it idea that just never seems to work.

What is something you lie to yourself about? You have to know you are doing it on some level. Do you think if you tell yourself a lie long enough that it will become the truth eventually? It just doesn't work. You will never be the "I'm fine," unless you do something real and tangible to get there. Not seeing something for what it is, really is, is only delaying the inevitable. Lying to yourself that you are happy and fulfilled, does not make it so. Lying to yourself that you will get to the gym tomorrow, won't actually get you to the gym. Lying to yourself that you have absolutely dealt with something and have moved on, doesn't make it true. It just means you have succeeded in lying to yourself.

I have a great friend who has no problem putting me in my place and calling me out when I need it. When he thinks I am not being totally truthful with myself, he will say so. We were having one of those late-night, existential conversations awhile back and I will never forget his face when he looked at me square in the eyes and said three little words to me; "You're not fine." We had been talking about everything that had happened in the past five years or so, and I was saying how I was worried about the effects it had on another person I cared about. I kept saying that I was fine with things, that I made peace and had moved on. He didn't buy it. Thing is, I really didn't buy it either. I had just been trying to convince myself otherwise. There are some things I have dealt with and moved on from and parts of the situation that I am totally okay with as they are. But, there are a few that I am not good with and I need to be honest with myself about them. I do not do weakness well and I refuse to let anything knock me down for long. However, I need to give myself time to heal with some other things that have happened.

I need to remember I am human.

The truth may hurt. It could strike through every protective shield you have in place. You may not *want* to hear it but you *have* to hear it. Never trust someone who lies to you, and never lie to someone who trusts you. If you make a mistake, own it. Feeling better about yourself is not gained by lying about someone else. It just makes you a liar. Trust me when I say that people will find out - they always find out - the truth, eventually.

Lying to yourself solves absolutely nothing. You owe yourself the truth every single moment of every single day. Sure, sometimes the truth hurts. But lies upon lies until you can't even remember the truth - hurts even more. You can't work on getting better, stronger or over something, if you lie about it even existing. Live honestly with yourself. You have to trust yourself and accept nothing less from the people in your life. Remember some people will tell you what you want to hear, so they can feel better. Trust in the ones who tell you what you need to hear, so that you can get better.

Live honestly.

LIFE SUCKS

Will you make mistakes? Of course. Some of the biggest breakthroughs I have ever had came from a mistake. Learn from them. Don't be afraid of them. Mistakes mean you are trying. Mistakes mean you are living again

"Life just sucks," one of my best friends proclaimed to me in a moment of frustration.

Yes, indeed at times, it does in fact - suck. I know this. You know this. Sometimes life resembles an evil merry-go-round and you simply go in circles of despair, frustration and hopelessness, over and over again for what feels like an eternity. You feel stuck. You feel lost.

You feel hopeless.

Your sleep becomes elusive at night, yet your exhaustion threatens to overwhelm you during the day. You stress eat or your appetite flees with your sleep and you find nothing tastes good or satisfies you. You make yourself constantly busy but seem to get absolutely nothing done. Anything to keep your mind off the simple fact that - life sucks. You dread the night. You dread those moments of free time with nothing to occupy your thoughts, for it is then your mind focuses on all that is wrong, but yet, never seems to come up with any way to make it better.

The evil merry-go-round continues. Round and round you go - where it stops nobody knows. Your shoulders begin to sag from the weight of it all. Your eyes become shadowed and downcast. You worry people will see failure in your gaze. You wear defeat like a cloak and become a shadow of who you were - who you want to be. You become a functioning robot. Locking your feelings down tight and letting go of hope. Over time you become to think that this is what your life will be like forever.

"Life sucks," he said. "Life is what you make of it," was my reply. He glared at me, thinking I was making light of his despair, I wasn't and so I continued on...

Life sucks you say. Yes, at times, it in fact does suck. Sucks bad. People hurt you. Circumstances that are beyond your control invade your life whether you want them to or not. Stress happens. Bad days happen. Hell, bad years happen. All sorts of bad happens. All sorts of good does too, but if you are so blinded by all that is bad, you will never see it. If life was constantly one perfect day after another, you would become complacent. Life would become boring and meaningless because you would stop trying to make it better. How would you appreciate all the good, being happy and amazing circumstances, if you had nothing to compare them too? You wouldn't. Your life is defined by what you do when the dark moments come. Your life is defined by breaking the cycle and finding your way out of the darkness. Your life is defined by YOU.

Yes life can suck. But, will you let that define you?

Honestly, in my opinion, the "life sucks" phrase is the biggest cop out I have ever heard. "I can't be happy - life sucks." I can't move on - life sucks." "I can't find my way - life sucks." "This person is doing this and making my life suck."

You can't find your way IF you don't get out of your own way first. You have to WANT to break the circle of the evil merry-go-round. Stop thinking and start doing. If sitting there in the darkness and letting your mind go to all that is wrong is getting you nowhere, then maybe it is time to stop. Don't think about changing. Actually change something. You can't move on because you keep stopping yourself. Figure out why and you will figure out a way to make it happen. Understand you can only control one thing in this world — yourself. Focus on that. Let go of trying to control others. Either change the way you think about a situation, change the way you handle it or just remove yourself completely. Forget trying to change anyone else. It never works and you will drive yourself crazy in the process. Learn to let go of what you cannot change and focus on what you can.

Life is what you make of it.

But it's so hard. But I don't know where to start. But I don't have the money. But no one understands... But-But-But. But nothing.

People do not need to understand and you do not need to convince anyone of anything. Yes it's hard; nothing worthwhile in life is ever easy. You don't know where to start? Try the beginning, I find that is as good a place as any, and if you don't know where the beginning is - it is where you plant your foot, stop going in circles and change directions all on your own - that is the beginning. Where you go from there is totally up to you. Will you make mistakes? Of course. Some of the biggest breakthroughs I have ever had came from mistakes. Learn from them. Don't be afraid of them. Mistakes mean you are trying. Mistakes mean you are living again. No money? Well, guess what? Money does in fact not make you automatically happy and content. Money can bring another slew of problems and does not solve everything. Does it help? Of course. Do you need it to change your life? Not necessarily.

What you need is the drive to change your life. You need to want to change your life. You need to release the fear of what could happen and just learn to roll with it. If something needs changing - change it. If something needs doing - do it. If you don't know what that "something" is - keep trying things until you find it. There is always something you can do to start to break the cycle. Even if that something is allowing yourself to have hope - hope that someday, maybe not tomorrow or the day after that, but someday, you will find what makes you come alive again.

Learn to think outside of the box. Try something new. Investigate life and spend the time you would have dedicated to thinking about why life sucks, to finding ways to make it suck a little less. Ask for help - it is not a sign of weakness. Ask for ideas. Google it for crying out loud. Do something. Become the super hero of your life instead of the damn villain. Don't stop before you start - just start. Somewhere. Anywhere.

All it takes is a single step to break the cycle. Feel the fire burn in your belly. Feel it travel up and ignite you to find your happy. Reach further than you ever have before because you deserve it. You and you alone are responsible for your happiness.

Life may indeed suck. It happens.
Now, what are you going to do about it?

FORGET CLOSURE - RECALCULATE

Each and every one of us who find ourselves in need of recalculating and adjusting to a new way of living, will one day break out of our protective cocoon and just as the butterfly – we will not only be changed, we will also be free

I was wandering through a quaint little store the other day when I chanced upon a beautiful dragonfly wall hanging, that quite literally, stopped me in my tracks. Instantly I thought of my mom and her almost childlike love of the dragonfly. I was transported back to a dust covered memory - of her sitting on the front porch giggling as what appeared to be a drunk dragonfly flew around haphazardly. With so many bad memories I cling to the good ones when they come. I felt my eyes tearing up while I stood there mesmerized by the wall hanging. Sometimes the loss of her feels like a gut punch when I least expect it. There had been so much bad but sometimes - there had been good too.

I chastised myself, as I walked out of the store, about allowing my emotions to get the better of me. It has been almost two years since she died, actually, the anniversary is fast approaching and I should have found some closure by now. Well, at least that is what people tell me - that I need closure. I need to move on. Okay, fine - to be honest, I tell myself this all the time too. Everyone always needs the ever elusive closure. People are looking for it at the end of failed relationships, after death, after loss, and well, after anything really that comes to an end.

Closure.

Honestly, I can't stand the word. The definition of closure is: the act or process of closing something. Closing something like a door or a road and not some huge part of one's life that is suddenly empty, hollow and shattered. You find closure when you leave a job and start a new one. You find closure when you pay off bills.

It was running into a road closure that got me thinking about life and finding the elusive closure.

Picture this; you are driving your normal route to work, you go to make the same right hand turn you have made every day for 10 years, and you are greeted by a ginormous sign that reads "Closed." You wail. You get angry. It throws a wrench into your entire morning. Then, you accept it as fact, recalculate your route and you continue on. Know what? Same basic premises apply in life too.

There are so many circumstances in life when you will never find closure. How could you really? Closure means you are no longer affected by something. Closure means you have forgotten the pain, the heartache and have healed completely. Maybe some people can. Maybe some people can cauterize a broken heart, can cement in a hole in their life left by someone they loved. Maybe they can - doesn't mean that you have too.

After finding that detour and having to figure out a new way to get to work - it dawned on me. You don't suffer a big loss, an ended relationship or death of a loved one and POOF! One day find that you are over it. You just don't. It doesn't work that way. Regardless of what people tell you need to do or how you just need to find some closure and move on.

Forget finding closure. Instead, focus on recalculating.

Recalculating. When a sudden loss occurs so does a shift in your reality. Whether you wanted it or not, your world changed the second it happened. Be it the moment your divorce was final, the last breath of a loved one or whatever the life event, when it happened - your reality changed. You must give yourself time to grieve. You must allow the tears to flow, the anger to rise and the full gamut of emotions to run their course.

You will feel totally out-of-control and helpless. You will feel lost and insecure. You will want the pain to end, the sadness to depart and you will want to feel the joy of life again. But, because closure is so incomprehensible, you stall out. Stop thinking about closure.

You may never be ready to let go of some of the sadness, you may never fill the empty hole someone left behind. You don't have to. Recalculate your life to acclimate to your new reality and go from there. This is now your starting point. Your go forward point. Make the needed adjustments and give yourself permission to move on. By acclimating to your new reality, by embracing your loss and making some form of peace with it, you allow yourself the first steps of moving on.

As I write this, I find I am visualizing a caterpillar.

The caterpillar is who I was before losing my mom. Actually, in the past few years I have lost a lot and my reality has shifted, re-shifted and shifted again every time. I realize I have pulled myself, like the caterpillar, into a cocoon of sorts. A protective shield. I know now that after a period of time - I, like the caterpillar, will decide when I am ready to break free. However, it won't be because I have embraced closure. It will be because I allowed myself time to acclimate to my new reality. That while I may still feel sadness, I will feel the pull of life even more.

Each and every one of us who find ourselves in need of recalculating and adjusting to a new way of living, will one day break out of our protective cocoon and just as the butterfly – we will not only be changed, we will also be free.

WORDS LEFT UNSPOKEN

When old age sets in and I am nearing the end of my time on this earth, I know I will have regrets. I am human. But, I will also know I tried as best I could to lead an honest life. To touch the lives of both stranger and friend. That those I loved - knew it with all their heart and those I had lost along the way would always know I had a special place in my heart reserved just for them. I had loved. I had lost.
But in the end - I won't regret one single second of it.

We are told to never miss opportunity. To never miss a chance, a possibility or leap of faith. That we must live our lives to the fullest so when we reach the end we have no regrets. We must live and love. We must reach out and touch others. We must go on adventures and try things that scare us. We must open new doors when one closes and reach for the moon - so if we miss we shall land among the stars. We must do good whenever the need is there and never miss the chance do to more. The fear of not getting to everything we want, not seeing-doing-feeling every single possible thing life has in store for us, the fuel to keep us going. When our time comes to leave this world - we must do it free of regret.

Impossible.

I know I have done a lot of things right in life. I also know I have done a lot of things wrong. I have missed opportunities. I have missed chances. I already have regrets. Some I can do something about, and others - I can't. I regret not going to college right out of high school. I regret not being able to help everyone I have wanted to. I regret not trying harder in certain situations. I regret not letting go sooner in others. I regret not following my instincts at some very key points in life. However, what I regret the most is all the times my words failed. Words spoken for sure, but more so, those I let die upon my tongue.

I regret words left unspoken.

One would think I, as a writer, would have always held a solid grasp of the power of my words and honestly, I do, but yet when I look back over the course of my life - I see many times when my words failed. Sure, words spoken in anger are always what come to mind first and foremost. Words, which the second they leave your mouth, you regret. I may have a few of these moments. Or words you spoke that were not completely the truth but were what you thought you needed to say at the time. Like the time I told my grandmother how amazing her green bean casserole was - it wasn't. However, she cooked it a bunch of times after that because she thought I loved it. In hindsight, I should have been more honest. Nicely of course, but truthful nonetheless.

Words hold so much power.

The power to leave your mind through your mouth and enter the ears of someone who so desperately needs to hear them. The power to right a wrong. The power to heal. The power of all that is you - within them as they touch the heart of another. It is these words I regret not uttering sometimes. When instead of telling someone I cared about how much I loved them, how much I needed them, I let the words wither and die on my tongue. The times when I should have said the words they needed to hear and put my own fear aside. Times when the power of my word was the only thing I had to offer and yet, never did. I regret the moments when I have allowed my words to stay trapped, repeating them to myself only, over and over again, instead of standing on the closest soapbox and making a sweeping declaration for all to hear.

I regret those times when my words were needed to stand up for something I believed in but I didn't believe in myself enough to say them. Those times when instead of using courage to bolster my words, I let fear quell them. Times when I let people walk away without ever knowing how I felt or when I walked away leaving my words trapped in my throat. All the things I should have said but never did. All the times I should have fought harder or spoke with my heart but didn't. I regret those.

What I don't regret is learning to see the beauty of always speaking my heart. I don't regret telling my friends how much I love them or my younger sister how proud I am of her. I don't regret learning to say things that need saying without fear of being vulnerable. I may regret all the times in the past, but I will not have the same regrets in the future.

Life is simply too short. Stop holding on to words that need to be spoken. Stop allowing yourself to let them stay trapped in your mind. If you have the chance - take it. Be honest with those you care about. Good or bad. Speak the words of your soul. Those words are the spark of your very existence. Speak them now or forever hold your peace. Though in my experience - that peace is elusive and the regret of not opening your mouth - holds strong.

When old age sets in and I am nearing the end of my time on this earth, I know I will have regrets. I am human. But, I will also know I tried as best I could to lead an honest life. To touch the lives of both stranger and friend. That those I loved - knew it with all their heart and those I had lost along the way would always know I had a special place in my heart reserved just for them. I had loved. I had lost. But in the end - I won't regret one single second of it.

Speaking my truths will be one regret I shall never have while living this amazing life.

Does someone need to hear your words?

Say them...

AGAINST THE TIDE

After one fights the tide and sees themselves through the storm, they will notice that even the ocean plummets and crashes - but it always leaps back up again, retreats in on itself, and gathers its strength to try again.

As I make my way down the narrow path that leads to the sea, walking gingerly in my bare feet, I can taste the saltiness of the air on my tongue. Tall dune grass whips in the breeze against my legs and I feel my heart start to race as my ears pick up the roar of the ocean. Fragile fragments of washed up shells litter the ground and I feel them break apart under my feet. Coming to the end of the path and the beginning of the beach, I stop and close my eyes against the bright sun. Tipping my head back so I can feel the warmth on my face. Breathing in deeply, filling my lungs with the air of the sea. Only when I feel my shoulders start to loosen, do I open my eyes and take in the cove. Sea gulls shriek as they fly by, swooping down to kiss the ocean and then blazing upwards over rocky cliffs that form the sides of the sheltered cove. I envy the gulls their freedom. My shoes fall from my fingertips to the sand as my feet guide me into the waiting ocean.

Tide is coming in.

Off in the distance, storm clouds gather; dark, fierce and menacing in their approach. The increasing power of the tide, a clear indication of what is to come. Though the sun warms my face now, it is clear that it will be short lived. I am fine with that. I have weathered worse storms. Walking further into the ocean I stop when it reaches my knees. My skin prickles at the sudden plunge into the cold water, and my feet sink down in the sandy bottom as the ocean comes forward and pulls away from me. Each wave that flows around my legs seems to have a bit more power than the one before. Slowly, almost imperceptibly, the waves grow bigger and bigger, until they reach the cuff of my shorts. Still I stand, simply allowing the power of the ocean to surround me. A shift in the breeze whips my hair around my head and suddenly the metallic smell of the approaching storm mixes with the briny smell of the ocean and the waves grow even more powerful. I square my shoulders and walk further into the sea until the waves reach my waist. The force of the ocean keeps trying to push me back towards the shore.

I resist.

This wasn't the first time I went against something powerful that tried to force what direction I went in. Wasn't the first time I didn't go with the flow and take the easy route to shore, either. In fact, most of my life has been spent swimming against the tide, facing storms, and refusing to change who I was in order to have an easier life. Sure, it would be easier to let the power of the tide dictate what direction I must go. But I wouldn't be who I am if I allowed it. It may batter me. It may knock me down to murky depths. I may float for a while to gather strength. I may just swim parallel along the shore line until I figure out what I want to do. The salt may hurl insults into my wounds causing them to sting and my eyes may burn with tears. But, I will still refuse to back down. Today, I almost dare the ocean to try and force me to shore. Walking further out until I feel that spark of life in my soul ignite. The ocean and life interwoven in my mind - both often leave you battered and breathless. Hopeless and cast away. But never doubt for a minute that while you can't control either the ocean or life, you can choose the direction you will go.

So, I go against the tide.

Hurts like hell sometimes and can be so lonely, too. But as I grew older I realized something - it had made me stronger and had taught me that being my own person, regardless of what others may think of me, is in fact, while hard at times, the most amazing accomplishment one can make.

It made me free.

When you stand strong in the face of adversity, when you face life head on and instead of hiding from it you confront it, you have no other choice but to become stronger. More sure of yourself in a world that is doing it's very best to make you follow along instead of doing your own thing. A world that is filled with people who will belittle you, mock you and shame you, for no other reason than because you are you. You will question yourself and begin to feel the world, like the power of the tide coming in, is simply trying to force you to conform and change against your will or drown you.

There will be days when allowing power of the tide to push you in the direction it wants you to go would simply just be easier. Why fight it? Why not just give in and let it all go? Why not just take the easy way? You tell yourself that you are too tired to go on, too broken, and too lost. The whole world seems to be against you and there is nowhere left to turn. Everything seems so hopeless and you just want to give up, your very being crying out to just let go. There is a moment, when you are at your very lowest, that you must make a crucial decision - do you harness the power of the tide or do you let it carry you away?

Standing there in the ocean in the face of the coming storm - I realize something. That with every wave I went through, every time I was knocked down and forced to swim back up to the surface with all my might and gasping for air, every time my eyes began to burn and my legs turned to jelly - I had made it because I fought the tide. The tide of loss, the tide of sadness, the tide of anger and the tide of hopelessness. It made me stronger than I ever thought possible and made me appreciate all the good so much more.

I learned a valuable lesson from the ocean...

There is an ebb and flow to life that is closer to the waves of the ocean than anything else. There are beautiful moments. Moments when the sun warms our face and the cry of the gulls warm our heart. Moments when all is right with the world. Then there will be moments of stormy and violent weather that threaten to destroy the very fabric of our hearts and minds. But after one fights the tide and sees themselves through the storm, they will notice that even the ocean plummets and crashes - but it always leaps back up again, retreats in on itself, and gathers its strength to try again. Over and over without fail.

All is not lost. Indeed, more is to gain when you learn to go inside of yourself to gather the strength you need to leap back up. It was there the whole time; you just needed the gentle reminder from the sea to remember.

DANCE WITH THE ANGELS

*I have faced demons and I have conquered. I have entertained the
emotional wraiths that have plunged my soul into the darkness,
only to learn to dance with the angels back to the light.*

I am not the same woman I was three years ago, seven years ago, 15
years ago, I have changed and evolved only to change and evolve again.
Finding out with each chapter in my life a little more about myself I never
knew before. I have broken. I have conquered. I have stumbled. I have
found my stride. I have made mistakes - so many mistakes. I have loved
and lost. I have watched the flame of life go out when loved ones passed
and have seen it rekindled with new life. I have faced demons and I have
conquered. I have entertained the emotional wraiths that have plunged
my soul into the darkness, only to learn to dance with the angels back to
the light.

I have learned there is good and there is bad. I understand now, one of
the biggest challenges in life is learning to accept that. I have learned it is
a balance and when that balance is out-of-whack, I must do everything to
correct it. I have learned avoiding is not the same as healing. I have also
learned holding on instead of letting go - can force your soul to be
chained to a rock deep inside yourself.

I have learned with healing comes change and change can hurt, I have
learned throughout the hurt and I have evolved, and throughout all of
these experiences - I have been becoming. I have learned evolving and
becoming requires acceptance and that I get hung up on this step way
more than I should. I am currently learning one will not flourish if one
keeps acceptance at bay. I have also learned exactly how stubborn I can
be. (I blame my grandmother for the stubbornness.)

I have also discovered you can do the above stages for any number of
things in your life at the same time and sometimes not even realize it. I
have learned problems can be a lot like nesting boxes. You focus on the

big looming one and decide it is time to work it out of your life - so you rip the top off, only to realize, so many other problems of varying degrees of difficulty lay nestled inside and the big looming one is actually comprised of all the others. It can be overwhelming. You are tempted to put the damn lid back on and bury it in the back of the nearest closet. But, you listen to that little voice that guides you, and you leave the cover off - knowing it is time to begin your journey.

Release and Heal

At various times throughout life when I was feeling strong I would pull things from the past that I had sequestered to some remote part of my mind and bring it out to the light. I would spend some time holding it in my mind and in my heart, examining it almost like I would a piece of sea glass, turning it over and over, holding it up to the light and just letting my emotions flow unchecked. Then, after a while, I would say my piece to it and bid it adieu. I would sweep away any remnants of sadness, anger or feelings of loss, and just like sweeping the floor of my kitchen; I would do a soul cleaning and be done with it. Occasionally, I would pull something forth I was convinced I was almost done making my peace with or making sense of, only to realize I still had some work to do with it, so back in the recesses of my mind I would put it. Knowing while this was acceptable for the moment, I must force myself to make an honest assessment of my feelings toward it and be firm with myself not to let it fester too much longer.

I also discovered, with certain things in life, I needed a bit more powerful and more cleansing way to find release. One day, while working through something, I wrote out on a piece of paper everything I could about this particular subject, then when I had it all out of me and onto the paper, I went outside to my fire pit and lit the paper on fire. I watched as all of the words which conveyed what I was holding onto - went up in flames. The release I felt was stunning and felt like cauterization of a wound, which could now heal on its own. Over the years, I have burned photos, letters and some mementos, and I have to say that after each instance - I felt lighter.

I am a huge believer in visualization. Sometimes, I will hold the image of a huge group of balloons in my mind - I visualize what I need to release - an emotion, a thought pattern, a memory and then - I attach it to a balloon and release it to the sky. Releasing whatever it was I was holding onto and feeling the peace as I watched it gently float up-up-and-away towards the sky. Another way I have discovered that works to dispel anger is to visualize blowing up a balloon. (Actually blowing one up works awesome too.) Close your eyes and imagine yourself blowing up a balloon by forcing all the anger out of you with deep, cleansing breaths. Once you have released your anger into the balloon, sometimes you may need more than one, tie it off and only when you can feel your muscles relax - **POP IT!**

Whatever you find works best for you, be it tangible or visual, releasing your emotions, releasing yourself from a bad situation, releasing yourself from the power of the past and its hold over you - is the first giant step towards healing. Holding on to something that hurts you, makes you sad or chains you in the past - does not serve you, your heart, soul or mental health, in any way. Releasing and healing will part the dark storm clouds and allow the light back in - preparing you for changing and evolving and moving on to next chapter of your life.

Change and Evolve

Change is scary. It opens doors to things in life we have yet to discover. Change forces us to look into the depths of our soul and find what needs to come to light and then actually bringing it out to the light. Change means facing fears and conquering them. Change means taking risks and opening ourselves up to hurt and possible failure. We can't wrap life in bubble wrap and we can't expect to never get dings and cracks in our souls, because life is going to ding you up once in a while, whether you want it to or not.

Some people in your life may react differently to the changes you make; they may not understand or accept them. So what? They are not living your life - you are. They are not your responsibility. Changing and evolving your way of life, way of thinking, way of handling or dealing with situations and you will be changing your entire world for the better. The further you evolve, the more you allow yourself to heal, and the more you change - the happier and more content you become. Add it all together and you find a strength you never realized you possessed and optimism for a future you once thought was impossible.

Become and Accept

With release comes healing. With change comes evolving. All leads to becoming and accepting your authentic self. Honoring exactly who you are and being free to pursue who you want to become. Those who chose to release the bindings of the past, freeing themselves from the shadows of their life and allowing the light and happiness to come back in - become an honor to themselves. When we honor all we have accomplished, all the roads we have walked and mountains we have climbed, we begin to understand in our very soul - all of the lessons, the dings and the heartaches, have given us the very foundation we need in which to become exactly who we want to be. We all have our starting points to become exactly who we were meant to be.

You just have to release the shackles holding you into place.

Everything in life has led you to this moment. Feel the power inside your soul to become whoever you want to be and feel the freedom to live authentically. Understand you do not need the world's acceptance of the changes you have made. However - and this is a big one - you have to accept yourself. All of yourself. The parts that still need some work. The parts you are still healing and evolving. None of this will happen over-night. It is a journey. However, during your journey through life and amid all of the changes, learn to accept every single new discovery you make about yourself, hold them close and feel the growing strength radiate from your very core.

Begin an adventure to discover more of your gifts and start to set goals of where you want to be.

The more you release and heal, the more you change and evolve. The more you change and evolve, the more you become. You become happy, content, challenged and hopeful. You become filled with radiating light and the shadows in your eyes become a distant memory. You become grounded and strong. Self-confident and sure. The powerlessness of yesterday has become the power of today. You become more trusting of yourself and excited about all you know you are capable of becoming.

You accept life will be different from here on out. It will be different, amazing, terrifying and exciting.

Then - You flourish.

NEVER SAY YOU'RE SORRY

I will not apologize for being confident. I wasn't always. But, once I stopped worrying about being liked and worried more about being me - life changed. I won't apologize for discovering my inner power. I won't apologize for learning, for growing or for finding my true calling in life. I will never apologize for fanning the spark within until it roared.

I will never apologize for being me. I will never apologize for being strong, smart or motivated. I will never apologize for living in accordance with the morals, ethics and standards that I have for myself. I will never apologize for attaining goals I have set. I will never apologize for not making the same mistakes as others. I sure as hell will never apologize for having my life together and for being happy.

I won't apologize because I don't have to.

I have made mistakes. I have had many, many missteps and direction changes. I have had broken hearts and shattered dreams. I have had my life reduced to rubble more times than I can count and yet somehow - always found a way to piece it back together.

I will not apologize for that either.

I will not apologize for my dreams or my dedication to make them come true. I will not apologize for my inner fire or my presence. I will not apologize for the material things I have acquired - I have worked hard for everything I have and am not ashamed of it. I will not apologize for being dedicated and will not apologize for any successes this brings forth. I will not apologize for my personal failures - I will however own every single one of them and find ways to do better.

I will not apologize for my decisions - if they were wrong I will admit it and move on. I will not apologize for keeping my stride when times are tough and will not apologize if I stumble either. I won't apologize for being outspoken. I won't apologize for standing up for something I think is right. I won't apologize for changing my mind when presented with new evidence or ideas. I will not apologize for having an open mind. I will not apologize for taking every person who walks into my life as they are.

I will not dull who I am because someone has a problem with it. I will not allow my actions to be dictated by another. I will offer no explanations, excuses or justifications to anyone who judges me and my life. Especially if they know nothing about me.

If I want to live my life out loud - then that is exactly what I am going to do.
Why?
Because I can.
Because I want to - have to - deserve to.

I will not apologize for being confident. I wasn't always. But, once I stopped worrying about being liked and worried more about being me - my life changed. I won't apologize for discovering my inner power. I won't apologize for learning, for growing or for finding my true calling in life. I will never apologize for fanning the spark within until it roared.

All of these things I refuse to apologize for... You shouldn't either.

If you allow the opinions and proclamations of others to determine your worth - you are doing nothing more than selling yourself out. If you listen to the nay-sayers, the disbelievers, the jealous ones and not to yourself - how will you ever reach your dreams? How will you fan your inner flame to a mighty roar if you let others continually blow it out? Stop apologizing for being you.

Never say you're sorry when you have done nothing more than honor your authentic self.

However, living this way does in fact come with a price tag. The more you shine, the more your inner flame roars - the harder some try to blow it out. Instead of owning their personal responsibility and focusing on ways to better themselves - they instead focus on ways to make themselves appear better by trying to make you look bad. Forget them. In school, at the office, within your family and friends or simply someone unhappy and miserable in their own lives - when someone is threatened by your life, by your successes, achievements, happiness and contentment - this is their problem - not yours. NOT YOURS. Stop letting this poison into your life and get back to being all you want to be, dream to be and will be.

Forget the nay-sayers.

I think turtles have it figured out. Soft on the inside, hard shell on the outside and willing to stick their necks out to get anywhere they want to go. So dream big. Live-out-loud. Never apologize for your triumphs or your failures. Never listen to those whose own unhappiness forces them to lash out at you. Forget their words. Forget their accusations. Forget the need to prove yourself to them. They will never listen because in truth – it is not you they are mad at. They are mad at themselves for never following through on their own dreams. For not living authentically. For not having the strength to take that same hard look within that you did. They will forever hate your shine – That's okay. Let them. When you live an authentic, honest and brilliant life – you will light your own way and the way of everyone who believes in you.

Never – Ever – Ever - Dull your shine.
Fan those inner flames and ROAR!!

LOOK FOR THAT WHICH REPEATS

You have to learn to trust in yourself. You have to believe in yourself.
Screw the rest of the world and what it wants from you. What do YOU
want from you? Once you figure that out... Do IT!
Everything else will fall into place.

We sat upon a huge rock letting our legs dangle just above the surging tide, watching as puffs of sea foam fluttered around our shoes. For the moment, hearing nothing more than the crash of the waves and haunting cries from the passing gulls, I let the world slip away and simply focused on the rise and fall of the waves as they came ashore. It felt like stolen peace. Call me a thief, but I needed it. The woman sitting next to me did too.

After a few moments she peered at me from the corner of her startling green eyes and sighed, turning her gaze back to the ocean she said, "Why do I keep making the same mistakes?" I could feel the weight of each word as it left her mouth. Each spoken word heavy with defeat, wrought with self-loathing, and laced with a sadness that went straight to my heart. "If it is not abusive men then it is my drinking, and if it is not my drinking then it is spending all the money I have saved and not being able to pay my bills," she forced these words out of her mouth, biting each one of them off as she said them. Her jaw clenched tight as she fought the barrage of emotions threatening to overwhelm her, looking me straight in the eyes she said, "Why do I sabotage everything good, why do I keep making the same mistakes over and over again?"

"Why can't I get it right?"

I looked at her sitting there, a strong and intelligent woman, a woman who had faced some serious adversities in life and yet was still standing. A woman who couldn't be broken for she always found ways to put the pieces back together. She was strong. She was smart. However, what she wasn't - was trusting. She didn't trust happy. She didn't trust content. For whenever happiness descended upon her life, one eye was always on the look-out for the bad that had to come eventually. This was the way her life went. Though she didn't trust the good times - she most definitely trusted in the bad. She trusted it to always come. So instead of allowing herself to be blindsided by it - she brought it in herself. I think on some level thinking that if she brought the bad in then she must be in control of it. Never works that way but it is amazing what we can convince ourselves of when needed.

I know exactly how she is feeling as I am there myself with a situation I find myself in. A repeat of a life lesson I was sure I had fully mastered, but apparently didn't. Took me awhile to realize I was repeating some old habits and when I did - holy epiphany Batman! I was shocked and furious at myself. How could I find myself in a situation so close to one I had already been through? How could I have not seen it sooner? How could I have let myself so easily slip back into a pattern I swore never to find myself in again?

Apparently life decided it needed to test my resolve. A sudden pop quiz to see if I had fully embraced the life lesson. Did I make it a part of my soul? Did I fully absorb the knowledge? Could I put what I had learned to use? Well, it appears maybe I didn't. My friend hadn't either. Because if we had - we wouldn't be facing the same things over and over again and still not getting it right.

Life lessons teach us. Life lessons change us. We came. We fought. We conquered. Right? But, what happens down the road when something comes up that you should be completely prepared to handle - you've learned the lessons, you've earned your knowledge and are armed with a been-there-done-that attitude and yet, still make the same mistake as you did in the past? What happens when you fall into the same old habits, reacting or overreacting the same way, being blind to the truth until it was too late, falling in love with the same type of unhealthy partner or whatever behavior it is that felt like it was what you were supposed to be doing - but in truth isn't even remotely close? Did you forget all of the hard-earned lessons of the past or did you fail to trust in your knowledge of all the ways NOT to do something?

Why are we sabotaging ourselves and setting ourselves up to always fail? We don't trust in ourselves. We don't trust in our instincts or our gut and for some - we do not believe we deserve to be happy or content for any myriad of bullshit reasons. We convince ourselves that we deserve it. We go in circles because it is a pattern we are comfortable with – unhealthy or bad doesn't seem to matter. Why should things be any different? Why should I be happy? We ignore the warning signs and jump right in because at least we know what is coming and we won't be surprised. We got this because we had it in the past. It is a vicious cycle.

We need to stop.

Look for that which repeats again and again in your life. Certain situations that you find yourself in, lovers you choose, your coping mechanisms be they drinking, bouts of depression, or moments of undeniable rage. Look to that which repeats for this is the lesson you most need to absorb into your soul once and for all. It keeps happening because it is what you are bringing into your life by not getting it all the times before.

For my friend and for me too - the circumstances we find ourselves in are ones that we have faced more than once. Each time falling into old habits and pulling the shield of old fears around ourselves like a cloak. We handle it over and over again because we know that we can - we did before right? It is a bad we understand. It is a bad we beat before. It is kind of like stacking a deck of cards - if you always know what is coming next, you will always know how to play them but in doing so you limit yourself to doing better. You limit the highest possible levels in life that you could reach.

Look for that which repeats in your life. Ask yourself why. Why do you resort to destructive behaviors? Why do you allow your depression to control you? Why do you take toxic lovers? Why do you constantly let a certain type of person always have an emotional hold over you? Do not be afraid to ask these questions and be less afraid of the answers. Be truthful with yourself even if the answers are painful and, honestly, often times they are. However, the answers will highlight your weakest points and while no one ever *wants* to see them you *need* to see them. You need to address them. You are only as strong as YOUR weakest point and identifying it and working on making it stronger will only make YOU stronger.

Trust the lessons of the past will prepare you for whatever the future holds, and when faced with someone you know isn't right for you or when something you have faced before and conquered comes around again - do not sell yourself out because you feel like you deserve it. You don't.

"When will I get it right?" she asked.

When you weave the lessons you have learned into your very being and trust in yourself. When you trust in the happy and when you release the comfort of the bad. I replied. When you stop making the same mistakes over and over again because you do not feel like you deserve better. When you learn to take care of yourself. When you learn it is better to be alone and sure of your heart than it is to be with someone who hurts you. When you see your destructive behavior is only caused by one thing, the one lesson you still haven't gotten yet, and that is this...

You have to learn to trust in yourself. You have to believe in yourself. Screw the rest of the world and what it wants from you. What do YOU want from you? Once you figure that out... Do IT!

Everything else will fall into place.

ONE MISTAKE AFTER ANOTHER

Will you make mistakes in life? Of course.
Here's hoping not the same ones as you have in the past. New mistakes
are lessons yet to be learned. New mistakes are life's way of bench -
marking your progress so you can see how far you have come.

I have made mistakes. So very many mistakes. The path I have left behind me on my journey through life is littered with them. Pieces and fragments of things I should have done the right way and didn't. Debris of words left unspoken and scattered pieces of lost chances and missteps. My life is a culmination of my successes - yes, but, even more so, a culmination of the mistakes I have made. The successes gave me confidence. The mistakes - the mistakes gave me truth. The mistakes gave me lessons and those lessons made me stronger.

I left words unspoken, which in hindsight, should have been yelled out loud. I let too much time lapse between visits with friends. I have allowed inner wounds to fester for too long without attention. I have walked away and let fear guide my steps to imagined safety, when in truth, it was simply the easier thing to do. I have mistakenly trusted those I shouldn't have and not trusted some I should.

So many mistakes.

I have a ritual I do at the end of every year, for as it draws to a close, I never fail to feel a sense of nostalgia settle into my soul. I will spend some quiet time alone, meditate and run a "Life of Jenn" review uninterrupted through my thoughts. I review choices and decisions made. Spend time reflecting on the new friends I have encountered and old friends who have made their way back. Scenes of the past year will flash through my mind at odd intervals, like a video montage. I laugh, I cringe, I want to yell at certain memories and warn myself in others.

Hindsight.

I find I spend more time reviewing the mistakes than I do the successes - not to beat myself up over them, but to fully embrace the lessons. To absorb all I learned into my soul and life. Some of them, okay most, do not bring forth warm and fuzzy feelings. Some bring sadness, while others - anger. Some make me shake my head at some of the less than intelligent things I did, like not taking care of a knee injury for two months, which led to surgery and being laid up for twice as long.

One of the biggest lessons I have learned: I must take better care of myself. Both physically AND mentally. I need to fully understand taking time and giving care to oneself is not a luxury but a necessity. It is not selfish. It is not bad. It is reality. I can't help others if I allow myself to be broken, exhausted and overwhelmed. I can't give what I don't have and if I don't take the time to take care of myself - I will have nothing to give. This realization, honestly, was hard for me to grasp. Worrying about myself always seemed so wrong, so selfish. I have learned – it's not.

I have learned it is a mistake to remain silent and expect things to change. Speaking my words and calmly stating what it is I need or want and what I will not tolerate - is a right not a privilege. I have learned while it is admirable and an honor to speak up for others, I am doing an injustice to myself when I do not do the same for me. I have also learned I cannot expect things to be different or change if I remain silent. Silence can be seen as agreement and it is on me, and only me, to use my words.

One of the biggest mistakes I have made this year - thinking people should change because I felt it was the right thing for them to do. Their actions and life choices, while at times affecting me, were really none of my business. I can't make people do the right thing. I can't make people behave in an acceptable fashion. What I can do is change the way I react to it. I do not have to get caught up in their drama or allow myself to be affected in any way. I have learned through this mistake the power of releasing negativity from my life, negativity which should never have been there in the first place.

I have learned holding onto sadness and regret hurts my heart in ways I never imagined. I learned how big of a mistake it really is to focus on what could-have-been, might-have-been or the infamous, if only. I have learned denying my emotions is just as bad. I can say over and over again I am doing okay with losing my mom and grandmother - but saying it doesn't make it the truth - I have to actually feel it. Learning to release my emotions out to the universe has been one of the most challenging to date. It has also been one of the most rewarding.

I have learned with real growth in life there is sometimes real growing pains. Letting go of certain situations or behaviors which have no place in my future, walking away from certain people and letting go of that which no longer serves my now or future, can and usually does - hurt. I have seen what a mistake it has been constantly second-guessing myself in certain situations and learned the hard way – that listening to my instinct is always the best course of action. I have learned nothing is forever and it is a mistake to believe there is enough time for all the "some other days," I have uttered.

Learning to trust the good in my life and the successes is something I have failed at many times. I have worked so hard to get to where I am today and I need to appreciate all of the good, which I do - but - and this is a big but - I have to trust in it. I feel some days when everything seems to be so positive and exciting and happiness is in my heart, that I always seem to have one eye cocked looking for the bad to invade again. I have to stop making this mistake. I have to live fully in the present moment. I have to learn and fully accept the fact that I deserve the good. I have to learn to stop expecting anything less. Will bad happen? Of course. Will it break me when it does? Not a chance. I just have to stop looking for it and allow the peace I have worked so hard for - flow through every nook and cranny of my world.

I plan to start doing this ritual of self-reflection more often throughout the entire year. I find it healthy and motivating to review all the good and bad I've encountered, and to gently remind myself to keep looking forward. Identify what should stay and what needs to be brought forth into the future. I must never fear the dawning of a new day or New Year as both are chances of a fresh and clean start, without any mistakes or missteps, a brand new beginning, just waiting for you and all you can bring to it. Make it yours! Own your future and dare to dream, dare to explore and dare to take those first steps you keep talking yourself out of.

This is your future! It is the beginning of exciting possibilities! But, only if you decide it is time to participate and not remain a spectator any longer.

Will you make mistakes in the future? Of course. Here's hoping not the same ones as you have in the past. New mistakes are lessons yet to be learned. New mistakes are life's way of bench-marking your progress so you can see how far you have come. Mistakes make the successes and triumphs that much sweeter and make you - smarter, wiser and stronger.

Here is to your future!

May we make new mistakes and learn new lessons and may these mistakes lead us in the direction of our dreams. May we find the inner power to release that which no longer serves us and open our hearts and minds to the power inside of us just waiting to be released. We are so going to rock this year. I can feel it.

Dare to Dream!!

BLAME GAME

I cannot hold someone in my present responsible for the actions of someone in my past. I need to take each person, each day and each situation on its own merits and deal with them accordingly. I need to release the knee-jerk reaction and take life as it comes.

Personal Responsibility: Owning everything single thing about your life, your actions or inaction, your choices, beliefs and history. Stepping up to the plate of life and saying loudly; "I take full responsibility!" Then, actually following through. It is taking control of everything you touch, do, say, or feel and honoring it. It is owning your mistakes, wrong choices, bad decisions and either making them right or doing better going forward.

It's in the moment when you stop blaming and start accepting.
It's in the moment when you let the excuse die upon your lips.
It's in the moment when you stop lying and start telling the truth.
It's in the moment when you realize that it's you who needs to change.
It is in all of these moments when your life becomes your own.

There was a woman with whom I was very close, and for years I watched as she placed the blame for everything wrong in her life firmly on the shoulders of those around her. Never once taking personal responsibility for any facet of her life. She would blame her children for robbing her of her youth, her husband for her unhappiness and various friends for never being there for her. She saw herself as taken advantage of and always felt let down by those she loved. She was a lost soul for so many different reasons - none of which being the people in her life.

She would blame the past for her present. She would blame her father, her mother, her sister and so on, for all that was wrong. She would cry and lament about the injustice of it all. Then, she would place the task of making her feel better onto her children. Expecting them to heal all that was broken and make life better going forward for her. She would place the responsibility for her happiness on their shoulders and then blame them for her tears. She failed to realize it was she who needed to take full responsibility for her life and happiness; not her husband, her children, nor her friends.

She never took personal responsibility for her life, and she eventually broke because of it. Until the day she died, she blamed everyone else for her decisions, her unhappiness and the life she never felt she had. She found scapegoats and excuses far easier to handle than taking the long and arduous journey of self-discovery. She never took control of herself long enough to understand the importance of standing on her own two feet and facing life head on. She never felt the pride of confronting her past and making peace with it. She never felt the feeling of accomplishment when she corrected a mistake or a bad decision. She never released the need to blame others for all that was wrong and thus - never took initiative to make things right on her own.

She was simply a bystander in her own life.
She never realized she had the power all along.

We all have things inside of ourselves we wish were different. We all have stories we wish we could go back and change or fix. Hindsight kicks our collective butt every chance it gets and we feel powerless. We feel the need to play the blame game because blaming someone else for all that is wrong is far easier than looking at ourselves.

I am no different. A sudden epiphany for me the other day revealed I was reacting to a situation badly, and instead of stopping and understanding why I was reacting the way I was, I placed the blame firmly where I felt it belonged - on my mother. Because of growing up with a bi-polar mother I have found that certain situations trigger an emotional response which has nothing to do with present day and everything to do with my feelings toward my childhood. I realized with sudden clarity - I needed to release it. I cannot hold today responsible for yesterday. I cannot hold someone in my present responsible for the actions of someone in my past. I need to take each person, each day and each situation on its own merits and deal with them accordingly. I need to release the knee-jerk reaction and take life as it comes. You can't blame anyone else for how you handle any given situation.

We all draw from a wealth of experiences. From lessons we have learned, mistakes we have made and directions we chose to take. Ultimately, we made decisions, wrong or right, based on what we felt we needed to do at the time. We need to own them. We are not made of Teflon; the blame does not slide right off from us and on to the person we feel should own it. In essence, when we do so, we are handing all of our personal power to another person. Think about that for a minute. When you place the blame on someone else - you are negating all of your personal power and giving it to them. You are saying to yourself - they have more power over my life, my thoughts and my decisions than I do. I have no control over anything and they have total control.

Why would you want to do that?

When I make a bad decision, handle a situation poorly or allow my past to dictate my future - I can't blame anyone for it BUT myself and while it may be uncomfortable saying I am sorry or taking steps to correct a wrong, I have to face it because I was the one who did it. If I go out and over indulge at dinner and get a tummy ache - who am I going to blame? The waiter? The chef? Well, unless they were at my table force feeding me, no. I am going to blame my lack of will power. I am going to blame my hand for continually raising the fork to my mouth. Of course, at first, I may blame the fork - I am human after all.

Stop holding today hostage for yesterday. Stop blaming everyone else for things you have control over. If you need to be a better person - be a better person. If you need to change your lifestyle - change it. If you need to do some work on your life or situation in order to get where you want to be - do it. Stop blaming someone else and start taking responsibility for your life. If you don't like what you see when you take an honest look at yourself - own it. Own it then work on making changes.

You had the power the whole time. Use it.

RUMOR HAS IT

*Worry less about what others say about you and more about what your
actions say to the world. Live your life so that your work, your heart and
your soul - shine. Live your life with honor and with integrity.
Live your life according to what YOU want to see, touch and accomplish.*

I was sitting across the booth from a friend of mine at a local coffee shop
awhile back. She was obviously nervous and worrying about something
and I could see from her eyes she needed to get it out into the open. She
was oblivious to the clinks and clanks of coffee cups, the aromatic smells
of fresh coffee and freshly baked muffins, things she normally cherished.
Something was eating at her and finally, after summoning her courage,
she blurted it out. A rumor she said - about me. A nasty, not nice at all,
rumor and she wanted me to know about it. She didn't believe it. In fact,
she got into quite the verbal altercation defending me. She was furious on
my behalf and then, upon seeing my face, totally bewildered. Bewildered
because my response was a deep belly laugh. A laugh so loud the other
patrons turned to look.

Of course I laughed, what she had just told me was ludicrous. A malicious
rumor of course, but hysterical in that there were some who just may
believe it. I giggled harder. She looked more and more perplexed.
Reaching across the table to touch the top of my hand, she asked me,
looking very concerned; "Are you in the process of losing it right now?"
Me lose it? Hardly. I was laughing at the sheer lunacy of what was being
said, and because I knew, without any doubt, who had said it in the first
place.

Wasn't the first time she had made sweeping declarations about me, my
character, my life or my decisions. Probably wouldn't be the last either.
She had been at it for so long now; I had stopped getting angry or
worrying about it long ago. The person behind this rumor liked to think
she knew more about me than even I did. This was comical, because in
truth, we have never even had a conversation longer than a few seconds.

But, because I live in a small town and social circles seem to overlap whether I want them to or not, she tended to disparage me whenever she got a chance. I will never understand why. I won't spend any time on it either. It is what it is.

People talk about you all the time and unless you are Mother Teresa (I'm most definitely not), what they say may not always be positive or make you look like the awesome human being you are. I won't say what comes out of other people can't hurt you - it can. Words are incredibly powerful. I also won't say the people in your life will necessarily not believe what they hear, some will. Some will take the words of another and judge you, sentence you and use them against you if given the chance.

What I will say - you don't need these people in your life. At all.

What other people think about you - is none of your business. Not in the least bit. Their thoughts about you are nothing you should ever concern yourself with, change yourself over or allow to interfere with your life. Why you ask? Simply put - doesn't matter.

What people think about you is less of a true representation of who you are and more of a direct reflection of themselves. People who have little to no self-confidence, a heart full of hate or jealousy, will project that out to the world and onto others so as to make themselves feel better. It never works for them and can turn into a vicious cycle. The important thing to remember - it is not a cycle you need to concern yourself with. It is not a battle you need to fight, because what they think and say - doesn't matter. What they think and say about you only hurts if you let it. You have the power to deflect it back to the source and bother yourself with it no more.

You have had the power all along.

Worry less about what others say about you and more about what your actions say to the world. Live your life so that your work, your heart and your soul - shine. Live your life with honor and with integrity. Live your life according to what YOU want to see, touch and accomplish. If people don't like it. If people don't "get it." Well then that's their problem and not yours. Let them talk. Let them say what they will because it won't change anything you have done or will do in the future. Let them talk because while they are busy talking, you are busy living. Step away from the shadows. Step away from the walls of fear and step into the light. Shine.

As long as you understand yourself. As long as you know who you are on the inside. As long as you continue to live authentically, no one - not friends or family - will ever be able to take the peace you have worked so hard for away. Because it is not theirs. Never was. It is their limited capacity to see beyond themselves, to what they need to change to feel better about their existence, that holds them back - not you. Never was you. I know it is hard not to take it personally but it never was about you. Those who speak horrible things, judge you or blame you for all that is wrong in their lives - have absolutely no place in your life or and maybe most importantly, in your thoughts. I don't care if they are family. I don't care if you have known them since forever - If someone is constantly trying to bring you down, make you look foolish or out to be anything you most definitely not - shut them down. Don't play into them. Don't bother to try and change their mind. That is not your job.

Your job – Well, your job is to the live as you see fit. Your job is to honor yourself. Your job is to let your confidence roar and your light shine. So many will bask in your light and see you for exactly who you are. Those friends who will believe in you no matter what - cherish them and hold them close.

The others - well, just know that by living happy and authentically, is all the justice you will ever need. Don't give them another thought. They do not deserve to be in your world, mind or consciousness. Laugh it off because you know without any doubt – you do not need anyone's approval to shine.

I Wish I Could Be Just Like...
Well, Me

Did you know it takes the exact same amount of effort to beat yourself up mentally than it does to encourage and believe in yourself? Did you know the only voice your soul needs to hear in order to flourish - is your own?

Repeat after me - **OUT LOUD!!**

"I am beautiful. I am worthy. I am capable. I matter. I may not know where I am going; I just know I need to take the first steps. My life is a journey and will test me at times - there will be moments that force me to bend but I-Will-Never-Break. I have been through the worst of times and though scarred, I am stronger for them. I will stop letting myself get in my own way and will be my own biggest motivator, confidant and friend. I will own my life as it is mine and belongs to no one - but me. If I fall down, I will simply pick myself back up. Because I matter. I matter to those who love me and those I have yet to meet. I matter to my community. I matter to the world. Most of all - I matter to me."

Say this part again - "I matter to me."

Did you know it takes the exact same amount of effort to beat yourself up mentally as it does to encourage and believe in yourself? Did you know the only voice your soul needs to hear in order to flourish is your own? Did you know there is not one single person in this world who will mirror your awesomeness back to you other than when you look into a mirror and your reflection stares back? You mirror your awesomeness every day but yet dull your shine and deplete your confidence with words of malice towards the one person in the world you should take care of the most - yourself.

I know what kind of a struggle this is. It was daily battle for me - up until the AHA! Moment I had one day while meditating on my life. It was a defining moment when I discovered I did in fact have something worth fighting for. I did in fact have something worth standing my ground for and not backing down. I had me. Me was all I have ever had, and if I can't count on myself in life, who can I count on?

So many look to outside sources to be their confidence, to boost them, when in truth - your biggest and best motivator never leaves your side. Your best friend knows you better than anyone else possibly could. Your best friend never-ever-ever leaves you. Your best friend is always there to pick up the pieces, apply love to the brokenness inside that no one ever sees and encourages you to get back up and try again. However, for most people, this best friend is often the last place they look to for anything. Would you like to meet this best friend of yours finally? I bet you would.

Go find a mirror and hold it in front of your face.
Your best friend in life is you.

Stop looking for validation from outside sources. You don't need to be validated by anyone in this world but yourself. If you continually wait for someone to give you permission to shine - you will wait forever. If you look to those who knock you down for no better reason other than to make themselves feel more powerful or better than you and take their words to be true - you are handing them your soul and giving freely of your own personal power. Manifest what you need inside of yourself. Believe in yourself, because it is not anyone else's responsibility. It is, and always has been, your responsibility.

Stop reading magazines and staring wishfully at the perfect models displayed in them, wishing you look liked this one or that. Just stop. Those models are looking back at you wishing they had the courage to eat a cheeseburger and to stop worrying about how they look. Those models have souls, hearts and dreams just like you. They want to be noticed, not only for their outward appearances, but also for who they really are. Just imagine, if you were to sit down for coffee with one of these woman to whom you are comparing yourself. Imagine her telling you how jealous she is of your freedom and how she wishes she would be taken more seriously for her thoughts and intelligence.

See, every single one of us is fighting the same emotions, the same feelings and the same enemy - ourselves. We talk ourselves out of reaching towards greatness. Who do we really think we are anyway? We tell ourselves we can't - when we really know we can, but are too scared to try. We convince ourselves we will most certainly fail, even when there is no way in hell of actually knowing until we try. We prepare plausible excuses and we play small. We are afraid of success even as much as we fear failure. Our comfort zones become more like prisons and we are trapped inside of a vicious cycle that takes possibilities and changes them to - never-will-be-unless-I-get-out-of-my-own-ways.

We have to stop being our own worst enemy. We have to be honest and truthful with ourselves. We must. How can you expect the world to accept you, believe in you and trust you, when you do not trust, believe and accept yourself?

We all have histories. All of us have had things happen in life that changed us, either for good or bad, yet here we are, still standing. Do you realize what it has taken for you to get to this very moment? You don't feel strong. You don't feel smart enough, pretty enough, capable or motivated. Look at everything you have already faced and made it through. Look to everything that has happened in your life. It hasn't broken you. Know what this means? Means it is time to believe nothing ever will because you are stronger than you think. You have made it this far.

There is only one thing stopping you now... You.

I swear I can hear you immediately come up with all the reasons why you can't in your head. Followed up by the words, she doesn't understand, I can't because of... or until... or when... I hear you because I often say the same things to myself. Until I make a conscious move to stop. Normally it goes like this; "Dammit Jenn, ENOUGH! Just stop already! Take a good hard look at yourself and then get over yourself."

The time to be honest with yourself and begin your soulful journey is right this very second. Silence the outside voices. Silence the voices of judgment that come from parents, friends, coworkers or whomever. Close your eyes and take a deep breath. Relax. Begin an honest examination of yourself, your life, your beliefs and your confidence or lack thereof. Look at your strengths and weakness. Really look. Look but - Do not judge! See all that you are, stand for and come from – just as it is. Because this is perfectly, you. Can you be better? Of course. You could be worse too. But who you are right this second – is perfect.

Identify your perceived limitations. Are they valid? Or could a change in how you look at them bring forth new possibilities or different ways of overcoming them?

Spend time with your fears - face them. Break them down to manageable bits and one-by-one confront them. Make peace with your fears and appreciate them. Allow them to dissolve because holding onto them does you absolutely no good.

Is there something from your past that has a grip on your soul? The time to let go and start picking the pieces up is now. I know. I know. You aren't ready. No one is ever ready. You won't ever feel ready. Stop over-thinking it. Stop putting it off. Stop finding excuses for all the reason why you can't. Stop thinking and start doing. Appreciate your story. Understand how it got you to where you are today. Then, release it. Whether you realize it or not - holding on to it is perpetuating the damage to your heart and confidence. By letting go, you are not invalidating your experience, for it is in the fabric of your soul, but you are releasing its power over you.

Our experiences make us who we are. Our experiences can also be a catalyst to reach for levels we thought unattainable. But, if you continue your strangle-hold on the bad, your hands will be too full to reach for the good. We hold on because we convince ourselves we aren't ready to let go. When in truth, we would like nothing more. Our fear and lack of confidence keeps us holding on because the future scares us. Opening up our heart and lives again, can be terrifying. But staying in the darkness is even worse. Appreciate your truths. Appreciate your past. Then release it in order to open up room for growth. More room for the happy, the evolving and more room to let the light back in.

While you are one of many in this world - you are the only you. You bring something to the world that no one else can. Your ideas, your thoughts, your love and being are needed because there is no one else just like you. Confidence in your abilities, in your heart and your appearance won't be found anywhere but within. It is only a struggle if you make it one. You don't need anyone's permission to shine. You do not need validation from anyone else. Their opinions in reality are just that - opinions. They are only true if you make it so. You have had the power all along, some of you have just forgotten. Learn to be comfortable in your own skin. Learn to value your intelligence and fortitude. Learn to appreciate your flaws because those flaws make you unique. Standing out is good sometimes. Blending in sometimes works too, but never sell your soul to be someone else or live someone else's life. To do so is a travesty to the very thing that makes this life worth living - you.

Your life - Own it. Believe in yourself. Stop playing small. Go big. Be bold. Find your courage and get ready to rock it.

Release your fear and... Live your life out-loud.

THE OTHER SIDE

You will get to the Other Side of things eventually. It may not happen in a way you ever wanted. It may not happen tomorrow. It may break your heart and your spirit in the process, but you will one day pick up those scattered pieces and build a life that you want. That you deserve and that you control. You may need to make some scary decisions; you may need to go out on your own, take some chances and Stand firm for what you want, what you need.
But, never doubt that you will get there.

The older I get the more like my grandmother I become. This in itself is totally not a bad thing, except she was always awake before the sun even thought about getting out of bed, and apparently I will be too. I wake up at 4 in the morning - every morning - whether I want to or not. I stumble downstairs, blindly find my coffee pot, pour my first cup and settle into my corner of the couch. When this first started happening I was really not okay with being up before the rest of the world. But, as time has gone on, I have come to treasure these moments of my day that are entirely my own. I don't have to be anywhere, do anything or take care of anyone. I am not distracted by ringing phones, laptops, deadlines or the busy that is my life. It is really the only part of my day until late at night that it is just me, my coffee and my random thoughts.

It was during one of these mornings recently that my thoughts decided to take a random trip down memory lane. The past is not something I visit normally. I lived it once and I really don't need to relive it again. But for some reason my subconscious - which is undeniably way smarter than my conscious brain - saw the need. Funny how when we stop distracting ourselves for a few moments what our brain brings forth to think about. It usually isn't something you want to be thinking about, but probably something you should be thinking about, at least for that moment.

I think what triggered this stroll down memory lane was an off-the-cuff comment a guy made to me during a conversation the day before. About people seeing who you are today and having no idea what it took to get you there. Every trial, life lesson, heartache and struggle you faced. His comment made me look at where I am today and step back to trace my journey here. For it is not just strangers who do not appreciate all you have overcome, but it is also ourselves who do not stop long enough, and occasionally pat ourselves on the back for what we have accomplished.

We made it to today. We made it to this very moment. For some this is a milestone in itself. Those who wake up in the morning and never know what the day will bring forth. The ones who wake up and only open one eye in order to peer out to the morning and see if the bad is waiting silently next to the bed. Or the ones who wake up every morning with a sickness, facing a day of pain, medications, doctors and procedures. The women who wake up next to their husbands never knowing which man will show up that day. The caring partner or the controlling, abusive monster? For some just getting through each moment is an accomplishment worth noting.

I have had moments in life when just making it through the day in one piece felt like I climbed the tallest mountain. When what I faced on a daily basis by all means should have dropped me to my knees, head bowed and arms thrown up, saying "I quit." But somehow - I made it through each and every one of them. Not because I am anyone special. Not because I have secret powers or magic cape - but because somewhere buried inside of me, I believed in the *Other Side*.

The *Other Side*.

When I was nestled into my corner of the couch, blanket drawn up around me and coffee in hand - I time traveled in my mind a bit. I was feeling anxious about the future and all the new things I have in my life now. Awesome things. Exciting things. Things I had only dreamed about were slowly coming to fruition. I was having a hard time believing in the good and that bothered me. See, I know where I came from, what I overcame, fought and dealt with, to get to this moment. But apparently I needed to remind myself the journey to the *Other Side* actually happened, I can trust in it.

Finding the *Other Side* took me more than 30 years. I didn't even know it existed. To me the *Other Side* was a myth. Mired in life, no hope for the future and lacking the ability to see beyond my now - even the thought that someday everything would be different, be better, would make me laugh out loud. The sheer craziness of the thought would have me shaking my head, dropping my shoulders and continue to solider on to what I was facing at the time. I didn't have time for fairy-tales.

I sat there that morning and traveled the roads that led me to here and now. From the philandering drunk father, to finding out when I was 21, he wasn't really my father, to meeting my real father and finding out I have five brothers and sisters I knew nothing about 10 years later. To spending decades locked in my mother's mental illness, never knowing day-to-day which woman I would get. And on through the years of unhealthy relationships, periods of self-imposed isolation from the world, bad decisions, and self-loathing. The tenacity, with which I hated myself for so many of those years, leaves me breathless. The losses, the battles, the never-ending cycle of bad that was my life.

I played my history like a video montage in my mind, seeing everything clearly as if it was someone else's story and, I, nothing more than a bystander.

When I came to the last few years I stopped for a moment. The sun was peeking through the trees and the quiet in my living room was calming. I sipped from my steaming cup of coffee and focused on its warmth in my hand. The past three years have been the culmination of all of it. The breaking point coming with my mother's death. The shock of her suicide, the devastation and the overwhelming urge to make sense of it all - was the final act. It was not as I wanted. It was not what I had envisioned. But it was the hand that life dealt me and I was left holding the cards with a decision to make. Do I hold? Do I fold? Do I play them?

I couldn't hold on to them. I refused to fold. So, I played them. What I won from that hand was - the *Other Side*.

So many of you are facing daily struggles that not many in your life see. Abusive relationships, depression, addiction, family problems and illnesses. Life. It can be so hard to see the end game because you are too busy trying to make it through the day. It seems never ending. It starts to feel like this is the life you are supposed to have and it will never get any better. That you are destined to suffer through whatever it is you're facing and that is just how it is. But take it from me, for it is one of the only things in life that I am 100 percent sure of - You will get to the *Other Side* of things eventually. It may not happen in a way you ever wanted. It may not happen tomorrow. It may break your heart and your spirit in the process, but you will one day pick up those scattered pieces and build the life you want. A life you deserve and a reality you control. You may need to make some scary decisions; you may need to go out on your own, take some chances and stand firm for what you want, what you need. But never doubt that you will get there.

When I finished my coffee that morning I realized with startling clarity something I had been missing all along. I had done it. I had found the *Other Side*. All the struggles, all the sadness and all the loss had led me here. I just needed to see it. I needed to believe in it.

Maybe you are getting there; maybe you have taken the steps to get to where life is good. Maybe, just maybe, you are already there and just like me - didn't realize it. Wherever you are on your journey, however bad or how hard a struggle it is - know in your heart and soul this one thing...

The *Other Side* exists. You will get there and you will be content. You will be happy and safe. You will feel the one emotion so many of us gave up long ago - hope.

Promise.

From the Author:

The cast of characters who have made appearances in my life so far are worthy of a Hollywood movie; I have had angels and demons, comics and drama queens, found loves and lost loves. I have been blessed with strangers who turned into lifelong friends and by those who only made guest appearances for a short time. Each one of them has contributed to my story - my life. Each one of them changed me somehow; good or bad and all have left their mark upon my soul.

Not only am I grateful for those who brought love, knowledge, laughter and amazing memories into my life, I am also grateful for those who brought heartache, tears, anger and strife, for both the good and bad have taught me.

For those who pushed me or pulled me, drained me or fueled me, loved me or left me, hurt me or helped me, all are a part of my story and to all I say - thank you.

A very special thank you to my husband, Marc and son, Trey. I never believed in love before these two guys walked into my world and never left, now I can't imagine a life without it. I am blessed. I would also like to express my deepest gratitude to someone who started off as a stranger and who is now one of my closest advisors, mentors and friends – Richard Szczepanowski. Richie has been with me from the very beginning of my writing career and without his incredible patience, constant cheerleading and skillful editing, I do not know where I would be. He has taught me so much and I am grateful.

I must send love and gratitude upon the wings of an angel to one more man. Larry Littlefield. Larry taught me to never play small. To honor all the strength, character and power I had inside of me instead of hiding it from the world. He showed me that being exactly who I am was exactly what the world needed. He brought me into a family, made totally of friends, who would do anything for one another. He taught me to trust – myself first, but others as well. Larry taught me to listen my instincts, to see the world around me and to be exactly as I wanted. His belief in me the motivation I needed to believe in myself. Though he is an angel now, he is always by my side. I was so blessed to have had him, even if only for a moment in time.

Finally, love and gratitude to all of you. The bond I have with so many of my fans has changed my life in ways I never thought possible. We laugh, cry, heal and evolve together. I wish for all of you peace, love, laughter and hope. You can accomplish everything and anything in life. I will always believe in you.

Lotsa love xoxo,

J. V. Manning

About

J. V. Manning:

Who is J.V. Manning?

She is at times her own best friend and at times her own worst enemy. Some days she has her stuff together. Some days she is a hot mess. She drinks way too much coffee, but always seems to be tired. She thinks a lot – probably too much. Her brain never really shuts off. She is quirky. She is a bit random. She is a tad bit crazy at times. She has been to hell and back and isn't afraid to write about it. She is a bit outspoken, probably too blunt and tends to speak her mind. She refuses to break regardless of what life throws at her. She likes to make people think.

She is the woman next door, the chick at the coffee shop, and the one singing in her truck at a traffic light. She is a wife, stepmother, sister and friend. J.V. is simply a woman who has seen both the darkest of days and the brightest moments that life has to offer and who one day decided to write about them.

J.V. Manning is the author of the wildly successful blog "Random Thoughts n' Lotsa Coffee." Her first book, "Random Thoughts n' Lotsa Coffee: A Collection of Writings Inspired by Real Life," was published in 2013.

J.V. lives in Gorham, Maine, with her husband and stepson. She can often be found down at the coast - coffee in hand - contemplating life while staring out at the deep blue of the Atlantic Ocean.

Made in the USA
Middletown, DE
16 April 2015